Real MOMS

MAKING IT UP AS WE GO

LISA VALENTINE CLARK

DESERET
BOOK

SALT LAKE CITY, UTAH

To Topher,

Miles, Owen, Phoebe, Hugh, and Margaret

Library of Congress Cataloging-in-Publication Data

Clark, Lisa Valentine, author.
   Real moms : making it up as we go / Lisa Valentine Clark.
      pages cm
   ISBN 978-1-60907-996-3 (paperbound)
1. Motherhood—Religious aspects—Church of Jesus Christ of Latter-day Saints. I. Title.
   BX8643.W66C53 2015
   248.8'431—dc23   2014045052

Printed in the United States of America
Edwards Brothers Malloy, Ann Arbor, MI

10 9 8 7 6 5 4 3 2 1

Contents

CONTENTS

iv

Introduction

Or, Every mom should write
a book on motherhood, and every mom could

Or, I'm not mysterious, but I always have lipstick

I have long held a desire to be considered a mysterious woman. I have fantasized about living a glamorous life in which I am poised, graceful, and well fashioned. A life in which people around me would wonder what I thought about ideas, politics, or art behind my big, dark sunglasses and simple couture dress. No one would really know, however, because I would be so mysterious. I would speak softly and intelligently in short, cryptic sentences that would be worthy to be mass-produced in large type and printed on canvas for display. Like Audrey Hepburn or Grace Kelly, I would never be without lipstick. I would never speak an unkind or misplaced word or have an emotional outburst. I would be mysterious.

I have, over the course of my life so far, become pretty much the opposite of that desire except for the lipstick part. I always have lipstick.

My husband, Topher, and I have a little game that we have been playing for years that just never seems to get old. Whenever we're watching a movie, we always identify the role that we think we would audition for or get cast as.

It's funny to us because we never cast ourselves as the lead character. I'm not even the "Wacky Best Friend" (I wish!); it's more like Cashier #2, who, we imagine, was just an extra who got pulled on set that day for a line, and I'm really excited about it because now I get paid for a speaking role. (My line is something like, "Will that be all?" or "Come again!" and I'm really stoked about it and I've called all my family and told them I'm in a movie!) Or maybe I'm the lady with the big glasses who yells, "He went that way!" as the protagonist of the film races by. (Topher will lean over to me and say, "You said your line really well," and I'll nod knowingly, as we both correctly identified the same character.) He and I can always spot our minor roles. We're middle-aged character actors. We know who we are.

We continue this same line of thinking with a game my clever book club friends play very well. Someone will say a funny or definitive statement about something—anything, really—that happened to them or that they've said, and then we'll attach their name to the end as the title of their memoir. Like this: I'll mention that my son has a limited palate and we don't know how he thrives, and Topher will say, *"Crackers and Cheerios: The Hugh Valentine Clark Story."* Or we'll tease our friend Patrick about his super trendy outfit, and then when he gushes over the food, fellow clever book clubber Josh might say something like, *"Hipster Ts and Melty Cheese: The Patrick Livingston Story."* Then we might imagine what our Lifetime Movie of the Week would look like. So, in that game tradition, I have jokingly referred to this book, written by Cashier #2 in the movie about motherhood, as *"Since Nobody Asked: The Lisa Valentine Clark Story."*

Every mom should write a book on motherhood, and every mom could. We all have those special moments when the ridiculous happens and we look around wondering, *Why aren't there cameras recording all of this?* We all find ourselves in situations no one could prepare us for—or, if they tried, we wouldn't have believed such things could happen to us. Like a classic sitcom moment playing out in front of us (minus the craft services and fancy dressing room) that no one is paying us to see.

You could write this book, and I hope you do because we need to share our experiences. There is value in having someone laugh at something that happened to you because there were, in fact, no cameras recording it. Our "live studio audience" wasn't there because that audience is the other moms, and we were all too busy running our own shows—so you're going to have to tell us about it. We need each other's stories. They help us laugh at ourselves, our kids, and our situations; they remind us to take a breath and move on to the next scene.

Motherhood is where we're hedging our bets. We've put our time into those things. We're in too deep to turn back now. All our eggs are in this basket. We've put in our 10,000 hours AND THEN SOME (thank you, Malcolm Gladwell) to be considered experts in our field. I walked away from a high school teaching career just as it started off to stay home with my first child, and I've worked on and off from home and sometimes out of the home in different fields. But no matter what I have and haven't done, I've identified myself as a "Mormony Mom who does some other stuff sometimes." It's over for me. Whatever I do from here on out is secondary to what I've been doing for almost sixteen years, and I suspect you're the same, no matter what your background or working status is. Whether you are a mom of little kids, older kids, or grown-up kids, a stepmom, a single mom, a married mom, it doesn't matter. This motherhood role has a way of ~~swallowing up~~ encompassing all the other areas of our lives. But the good news is that we're all in this together.

We talk about motherhood like it's a singular thing, but it's not. Some mothers have spouses, some don't; some have a great support system, and some operate under more isolated circumstances. Throughout this book I didn't separate my experience from my connections, and you can't either.

I got married at a young age, and it could have gone horribly wrong. I've read the statistics. We were both young and in love, and we didn't know how young we were, or we did and we just didn't care. Now it's nineteen years later, and it's still the best decision I ever made because instead of waiting until I got older, I got to be with him for that much longer.

Our story is the typical BYU-Boy-Meets-Girl story you've heard a million times: We were both in a really special English Society play called *Mysteries: The Creation*, about stories from the Old Testament, and he was cast as Satan and I was cast as a chicken. And Satan and the chicken fall in love after being friends for a year. Blah, blah, blah, tale as old as time!

I can't really separate my experience as a mother from my experience as a wife because my perspectives with each are all tangled up. I've now known Topher as long as I've not known him (and most of those early years when I didn't know him, I was a dumb baby and little kid, so they don't count). We've changed each other and we're a real partnership. It might be obnoxious to read, but it doesn't mean it's not true. We tell each other everything and we've been there through real life together: getting jobs, losing jobs, moving, living in England and Provo and Orem, being pregnant, giving birth, raising kids, changing careers, slogging through graduate school and more graduate school, directing plays, teaching kids to read and have table manners, and a million other big and little things. Being a parent is hard and it's wonderful, and I've always had a partner through it all, which has made it better. It's made it all the best, actually.

Topher is a really great father in a day and age when fatherhood is kind of dismissed as a bonus or novelty in parenting. It's often marginalized when we talk about motherhood, but that's not the way I feel. I talk a lot about being the kind of mom I want to be, and I couldn't do that without Topher. He doesn't try to change me, but he supports me in whatever I want to do inside or outside of our family goals. He has always respected the way I want to parent—more than that, he encourages me in doing the fun and the hard parts of mothering that he sees I want to do. He also values being a dad in a way similar to how I value being a mom, and I have found that very grounding and uniting for our marriage. He isn't dismissive about my pursuit of mothering. He is engaged, and he has shown our kids and me how important we are by consistently sacrificing time, money, and creative pursuits for our family. He loves it that I try to be the best kind of mom I can be—the kind I want to be—and he doesn't just tell me that, he rearranges his life to show me.

Being a mom has changed my relationship with Topher, whom I've always been crazy about because he is who he is. But now I feel such a deep love and appreciation for him that's hard to fully express because it seems too sacred or special to write down for everyone to look at. He's the father of my children and my best friend. Everything.

I thought about including how motherhood has deepened my relationship with Topher in the chapter "Shocking Moments in Motherhood," but it isn't shocking. Anyone who knows Topher knows that he's funny, intelligent, creative, talented, ambitious, kind, and generous. So when I talk about being a mom or about my experiences with motherhood, it's too hard to separate motherhood and fatherhood or me and Topher, so I didn't. Just assume that there, in the spaces between the text, Topher is right there with me through it all.

I know you're busy, so this book is a good one to read in chunks. You don't even have to read it in order (no one's the boss of you). It might not look like other books. I include advice you didn't ask for and some side rants, because I suspect you know exactly what I'm talking about. We're not overly interested in sleep theories, breast vs. bottle feeding debates, or discussions on organic diapers (please, no). This isn't our first rodeo. We are in the thick of it. We need advice specific to our particular kids and situations. We're in too deep for platitudes and theories. We need brass-tack talk. And this is a safe place to lay it all out, look at it, and pick up what is useful to each one of us.

Because, most of all, we need encouragement. We need a good laugh and enough rest and exercise and spiritual feasting to keep us going. We know the stakes are high. In fact, I think we're too aware that it all means too much. We Mormony Moms know where to find spiritual guidance, and we know the tools we need to help our kids. Oh, we know, all right, and it's all too much sometimes.

Every mom should write a book on motherhood because it's very humbling. It's a way to point out, with laser focus, our flaws amid our very, very good intentions. But it's also a great way to rededicate ourselves to the tasks at hand and all that we have to do and *get* to do by being the mom. Sharing our triumphs and tragedies may take away some of our mystery, but it's worth it in the end because what we're doing in raising kids is super important, but also a little bit ridiculous, which is funny. And all the moms I know, including myself, could use a solid laugh.

Besides, being mysterious is overrated. Or so I'm told. I really wouldn't know.

All the Things

Or, Go ahead and ask me what I do all day—I dare you

When I stop to think what is asked of women, I immediately think, "ALL the things."

We are asked to do *all of the things.* I have read far too many studies showing that although most women work outside the home, they are still responsible for the majority of the housework and child-care responsibilities. In my personal experience, I have seen several men walk away from family responsibilities, but few women (I know that happens, but certainly not as often). And as our responsibilities increase, we are increasingly told how to spend our time, money, and other resources.

For example, most people are obsessed with the way mothers use their time. You never hear some passerby mention to a friend who is, say, a lawyer, "Well, since that deposition is over, what are you going to do with all that time on your hands?" Or I'm sure business owners aren't asked about the use of their time after the holiday shopping season has quieted down. But you will quite frequently—alarmingly frequently—hear strangers, friends, and family members ask mothers, "Now that your kids are all in school, what are you going to do with all that time?" or "Now that you quit your job (or went part-time, or hired a cleaning lady), what are you going to do with ALL THAT

TIME?" And right there is one of the leading reasons we, as moms, feel the need to justify, fill, prove, and explain our time away to other people, when it's really none of their business.

Of course, it's really not that simple. Some of us suffer from disorders like "recovering perfectionist," or "recovering-overachiever-without-a-blue-ribbon-but-trying-to-figure-out-how-to-get-a-blue-ribbon-for-achievements-no-one-knows-how-to-quantify" (not a scientific term, but truly a debilitating disorder). Sometimes I refer to my own inability to live in the moment as I search for validation as "*antsinmypantsdisease*" because I have a hard time NOT doing things. Like I feel I need to be folding laundry while watching TV or helping kids with homework while making dinner and trying to write down notes for a project, all at the same time. This does not mean that I don't have days, and sometimes weeks, when it's hard to do ANYTHING and I don't feel like I've accomplished anything. There were some baby blues weeks (*years*) when showering was a major accomplishment. Someone with my disorder would, literally, make a list like:

❏ Keep children alive
❏ Shower
❏ Eat

And check off these items and feel pretty good about themselves. As they should.

Now my focus has shifted from keeping my children

alive to teaching them how to be good, moral, interesting, educated humans who can live and thrive on their own, independent of me. This focus, this "one thing," is really all things. As I take a dip in the middle-age pool, I'm realizing it may never have an end. So I can sleep through the night and shower by myself now, but I'm still interrupted all the time—although it's not like I have to listen outside the shower to decide if someone has opened the front door and is running down the street, or has opened the knife drawer, or has climbed on the roof (all of those things have happened to me while I had a "quick" shower). I need that sleep and a long, hot shower to get me ready for whatever's next because it could be anything.

But as my confidence and ability to accomplish more tasks daily has increased, so have the demands on my time. And this makes me super mad. I now know that the more you do, the more people will ask you to do. And the better you do something, the more people will take you for granted. It's a catch-22, isn't it? You're feeling better and you want to help everyone succeed: your spouse, your kids, your school, your church, your community. But they don't know *the other things* you're doing in addition to this "one little thing" they've asked you to do. Only you know the accumulation of it all, and so, once again, it falls on you to do that one more thing or not do that one more thing.

The world seems to assume that a mother's time is not fully her own. She needs to, or feels she needs to, justify her use of time to everyone, and that drives me crazy because not only is it insulting, but it highlights the subservient attitude others have toward mothers. We casually list achievements in conversation to justify our work: *Oh yeah, after finishing the laundry and hitting the gym, I volunteered in the classroom and then was able to send some emails for our family reunion and get started on dinner.* I have always felt it a privilege to be able to spend a lot of time with my kids, so when other people treat it like it's an expectation or an assumption, that seems to cast it in an ordinary light, which I don't appreciate. Notwithstanding my rant, I also think that one of the benefits of my opportunity to stay home with my kids for the majority of the day is the chance I have to serve in the community and school. But disrespecting my choice by assuming I don't have one is insulting.

I'm one of those uptight moms who

Side Rant

I will always think it is the greatest blessing that women have so many choices in this day and age. But as a mother, sometimes I get so sick of making all the decisions, I could scream: what to have for dinner, what brand of detergent to use, what to focus on as a family, what to do about retirement, what our policy is on sleepovers and music lessons and every one of a million little and big things!

really DOES CARE if all the beds are made or if there's popcorn on the floor, trying to pretend to be an easygoing, "whatever" mom. I TRY to exercise patience, but I have my limits. My limit usually reveals itself with trigger objects: a discarded candy wrapper on the floor or an unmade bed (all they have to do is pull up a comforter cover!) will send me into a fit. Exercising patience becomes an example of how, in parenting, I am doing a disproportionate amount of the work: So now I have to be PATIENT while they ignore me or treat me like the maid? Why am I the one who has to do everything—including CHANGE?! But, I'm the grown-up and I'm supposed to be modeling correct behavior.

One day, after days and days, turning into weeks and months, of entering the basement, where all three boys share a room, I decided I had had enough of the quiet teaching moments, and it was time to do something drastic. They always left their wet towels and dirty clothes on the floor in their room. Not only was it an eyesore, but it was really gross and smelly, too. I couldn't just "let this go." I had tried everything: I had explained to them why I wanted them to keep their room clean (citing logic, reasoning, and science); I had told them I would charge them a dollar for every day they didn't do it; I had cheerfully, no-big-deal, casually reminded them at breakfast before they left; and I had reminded them, ahem, loudly. Using my outdoor voice. And so, in a moment of what I thought was clever inspiration and an example of AP mothering, I wrote two big signs in Sharpie. One said, "HANG UP YOUR

TOWEL!" and the other, "PUT YOUR CLOTHES IN THE DRAWER!" I taped them right at the boys' eye level in the closet, where their dressers and the hamper are.

The next morning, confident that my skills were unmatched and imagining that I might now offer this gem of advice to all my friends and family (*in person or by email?*), congratulating myself as I bounced down the stairs, I was surprised to see the following scene: Under the sign, "HANG UP YOUR TOWEL!" were two wet towels lying on the floor. As for the sign, "PUT YOUR CLOTHES IN THE DRAWER," someone had flipped the sign over and written on the back with a ballpoint pen, "OWEN IS THE MOST WONDERFUL CHILD IN THE ENTIRE WORLD!"

When I confronted them, Miles, the oldest, explained that he had forgotten to pick up his stuff. "Really, with the sign and everything?" I asked incredulously. But, if you know Miles, you know that it really did slip his mind and that it wasn't malicious. He promised to do better. Owen smiled smugly and put his arm around me and said, "How'd you like my sign? I know that's what you meant to say!" He laughed and promised he would try harder, but he kept laughing, looking for my approval that his joke was appreciated. I said, "Just pick up your clothes, you guys. Got it? Message received?" and now they do much better. Okay, not much better, but slightly better. But I got the message: They don't care about towels and clothes.

It's hard to keep up with *all the things* because the master list is always changing. Remember when everything was fat free and it was healthy to eat baked potatoes (like, it was a diet food and everything) and eggs were supposed to kill us? And now the opposite advice is trending: white potatoes are the worst food in the world, void of any nutritional value, and are going to kill us; fats are good now, but only the good kinds, so read up on what those are and which ones to eat; and now eggs are back in and great for you. Modern mothers have to be well-read and informed about all issues, parenting and otherwise, like: Is it back or tummy sleeping for infants? (And what about when they roll over? Don't get me started on that conundrum.) We shouldn't let our kids walk home by themselves. No, now our kids should be free-range and use the bus and subway system confidently. We should give our kids opportunities when they're young, and their minds are sponges, to learn foreign languages and music. No, we should give children their childhoods back and let them wander the neighborhood and climb trees.

Not only does modern mothering require your decision-making skills to go into overdrive, but you have to have a reasonable amount of research logged to make these decisions no matter what you decide. Again, *all the things.* I read up and I listen to a lot of National Public Radio. (NPR has an effective way of telling me in soothing tones that the sky is indeed falling, but isn't it fascinating?) But there are still a lot of tabbed articles in the *New Yorker* or bookmarked online news articles waiting for me that I mean to read sooner than later, but I want to eat my fried white potatoes (still considered not healthy, FYI) and clean out my DVR, too, sooo . . . only so many hours in the day, people.

My sister Gina has a theory about the scarcity of time. She believes that moms can do more with less time out of necessity. She's realized that before she had kids it would take her all day to accomplish what she's able to do in two to four hours now that she has kids. "Before kids, I would dork around doing projects, running errands or whatever, and it would take all day, but now that I have kids, I can get stuff done super fast in less time. I wasted so much time before, but I didn't even know it!" Other artists and professionals don't wait to *be inspired* to do what they do, they throw themselves in it and make habits and deadlines. I suppose motherhood is like that too. We form a lot of habits and we get done what needs to get done (even if it's in the twenty-third-and-a-half hour). But because of this, it's hard to have down time. I always think "free time" is a trick, like I'm just forgetting something or I'm being unwise with this time when I could be prepping for something coming up, something I might (probably will) forget in the future because something will inevitably be thrown at me last minute because someone else forgot something or because that's just life. Down time is tricky. Modern movie culture tells me to sing into a hairbrush with my girlfriends and that will do the trick, but it just doesn't seem to be that simple for me.

There's the well-known list of things a mom does that we all frequently enumerate, which includes things like cook, chauffeur, housecleaner, etc., but add to that working, policy making, changing self-identity, adjusting personal tendencies and habits, researching, decision making, explanation making, and defending because they too are part of *all the things*. And even though I've complained about having to do *all the things*, I actually feel a quiet resolve to do them because I like to. It's not all bad. I want to be more Pollyanna than martyr about it. In general, being a mom is a lot of fun. I don't think about *all the things* in relation to what it means to be a mom; I think of *all the things* when I think about living life and being a grown-up.

I remember the day my oldest son, Miles, about fifteen months old, discovered the wind. He was toddling along and a big gust of wind came by and almost knocked him down. As he steadied himself, the look of delight and amazement on his face as he seemed to say, *What was that? That was awesome!* took me by surprise, and I knew that I would always and forever remember that expression. Miles has always been inquisitive and smart and full of humor, even as a toddler, and he always has funny or interesting things to show me—shows, books, articles—and he's still delighted by discovering these things.

Owen was a curious, fearless little kid, but never unkind. As a baby he had exaggerated features: a huge mop of dark hair, huge eyes, a huge mouth, and an equally huge amount of excitement and energy for life—and he's never lost it. I can still see his face exploding with excitement as he would run with all his might toward me as a two-year-old to knock me down with his hug. When I think about all of him, I think of his kindness to me, like when he shows me something dangerous he's done. He tries to do ten consecutive flips on the trampoline, for instance, and I protest about safety guidelines and start my speech about making good decisions, and he smiles and puts his arms around me and lets me say it and reassures me he's fine and asks me about *my* day.

I remember spying on Phoebe as a baby to listen to her sing when she woke up, memorizing her voice and face. Topher and I are still holding our breaths because she seems too easy to raise. I know she's not a teenage girl yet, but she is so happy and willing to look on the bright side of life and she makes our home such a happy place to be, and it's been that way ever since she was born.

When Hugh was born, he was really mad that he had to be a baby and a little kid. I remember a time when he would run, chasing the big kids down the street on their way to school and crying that they had left him. I would scoop him up and bring him inside and calm him down by reading books with him. We would lie there, and I would tell him that his little sister was inside my belly, and he would laugh because, well, *that just seemed crazy,* but he would play along and say "Hi, baby!" Then he would laugh again and check to see if I was kidding or not because growing humans inside your body is a joke, right?

I remember looking at Margaret when she was born and thinking she was so beautiful, like a doll. The nurses fought over who got to take care of her in the hospital nursery, and Topher commented in a teasing tone that he would love to have a little wallflower girl who would just stay near him all her life because the other kids' personalities were all so big, and that would just balance out our family. I think of her as a little three-year-old girl standing on her chair at dinner, trying to get our attention by retelling a knock-knock joke one of her siblings had told her, or singing "Poker Face" or "Bulletproof," and how the older kids don't let her just have it, but she has to work to make them laugh, and as a result she has some skills. And now she's grown up to be the biggest personality of them all.

I have a million little memories and experiences like these locked up in my heart, the accumulation of which is what being a mom *means* to me. Words won't do. Being able to see my children at every age, in every stage of life, and having the muscle memory record the feel of their bodies as I carried them, rocked them, hugged them, picked them up, washed them off, comforted them—it is all recorded and it has changed me physically and spiritually. Of course it has, and I'm so honored that it has. Of all the names I have, my favorite one is "Mom." It means *all the things* to me.

Phrases I Never Thought I'd Say:

"We don't fight with guns when we talk to Jesus."

"If I don't sleep, I will DIE. I'm sure of it. You're all killing me. Slowly. You're all slowing but methodically killing me. Good-bye, everyone, I tried."

"You have a PhD and you don't know how to buy SKIM MILK?! I feel sorry for you."

"If you finish that merit badge I'll give you five bucks."

"So you DID the assignment, but you just didn't turn it in, and you don't know why you're failing English? This is where we are?"

"I don't know how to parent you in this situation."

"No, I'm not running a day care, those are all my children."

Lowering the Bar and Being Awesome

Or, Motherhood is enough and we don't have to stage elves
in suspicious, menacing positions to delight our children
unless we really want to and in that case, carry on

Or, Stop making fun of our jeans
because that's not a thing anymore

Our job is a cruelly ironic one: We love, nurture, and teach our children to go out into the world so that they can live, function, and thrive without us. So they don't need us. Don't need our nest. It's cruel. It's a job that is revered and honored and, conversely, an easy target for the crudest of comedians. Sure, we get flowers and sweet homemade cards once a year, but there are also "Yo Mamma" insults and never-ending jokes about our jeans.

It seems that we all agree that our objectives as mothers are overwhelming, but so is the advice we give one another. The big dilemma of modern motherhood is the need to categorize each other, emphasizing our differences. Ultimately, we're told it's not enough to raise happy kids, we need to show our mothering to everyone, displaying it and telling everyone else how to do it too.

I think one of the reasons it's overwhelming is because we are asking the wrong questions when we get to talking in real life or online. Different media outlets, in order to sell stories; bloggers, to get comments and page views; and other parents, to make themselves feel better and further validate their own choices; all want to pit mother against mother with antiquated, oversimplified frameworks: working vs. staying at home, breastfeeding vs. bottle feeding, organic vs. FDA standard, public school vs. homeschool, and so on. We use these clichéd "hot topics" to test other parents to see if we're alike or not and to validate our own choices as mothers. After all, how can we prove we're a good mom *unless we're better* than someone else? It's mean, judgey, and not at all helpful. In fact, it's hurtful to our mothering community because it divides us and further separates us from each other in an already isolating, overwhelming job where the stakes are high.

This public judging and comparison comes with a price, but we haven't even had this technology long enough to really know what that price is. We can all guess, though: an overwhelming feeling of dissatisfaction that we're not doing enough, that we should do more, or do better, comparing ourselves to an unrealistic, fictitious portrayal, followed by anger, dissatisfaction, and disillusionment. Haven't we all had that moment where we've thought: *Hey, I didn't get a cute baby shower for my third child, with diaper-shaped cake pops!* Or, *So now we have to put an elf all over our shelves staged in suspicious, menacing positions to delight our children?! That's **a thing** now?* Or, *Oh, okay, they went to lunch together without me. Awesome, I didn't want to go. Took a lot of pictures of themselves, huh? I don't even like Zupas.*

What my own mother, who didn't live through this era, taught me about motherhood applies here: Motherhood is enough. And now my motto is *Lowering the bar and being awesome.* Not in a discouraged way, but in a realistic, individual, positive way. I don't want to regret this time raising my children, but only I can determine what that means to me and my kids. "Lowering the bar" is my commitment to reject the "tests" others try to put on me—and it may mean that I appear less accomplished than other moms. Maybe less put together or even less generous. It might mean that I appear flaky or disorganized, but it always means that I am responding to my kids' changing needs all of the time. And the last part, "being awesome," means just that—that I am happy about my choices because I'm living without regrets and "should-could-would-haves." I'm fully aware that I'm not cool, that I don't win, and that's awesome.

My own mother holds a radical religious belief that is not considered doctrine in the Church, but she and I believe it. It's this: She would tell us as children that before we came to the earth, as spirits in the premortal realm, when it was time to be organized into families (again, not doctrine), she jumped up and down and said, "Please, please let me be Lisa's mom! Oh, please—pick me!" That was how my mom *felt* about being my mother. And that was the first and lasting dialogue I have in my head about what being a mom *means*.

You should feel a little sorry for me because I have the perfect mother, but you won't. You'll be suspicious of me and that statement and you'll reason, *No one can get it right.* To which I'll reply: Hey, as moms, let's talk about "lowering the bar and being awesome," not as an apathetic "there's only one ideal and I'll never meet it," and not the illusive "good enough," but with a third definition, "fit for a specific need." Let's take back the word *perfect,* not assigning to it the meaning "without flaws or shortcomings," or "beyond improvement," but a third meaning, "exactly fitting the need in a certain situation or for a certain purpose."

So why do I want a little sympathy from you? Because every day in raising and caring for five children, I know better. I know what I should be doing. It's not elusive, and I can't pretend it's not possible to do a good job. My mother taught me that I am enough for my kids. They want *me:* my time and attention, my energy, love, silliness, education, and so on. I don't get caught up in competition (for the most part—I *am* a little more type A than I generally like to admit) because I want to be the best for my kids: perfect for them. That's another reason why my mom is nearly perfect—she prepared me for this environment of mothering before it even existed by showing me what were the most important elements of mothering.

When I was growing up, it wasn't uncommon for all the neighborhood kids to congregate at our house. Regularly, they would come before school and after school, and it became apparent to me that my mother was being taken advantage of. I confronted her about this and said, "Doesn't it kill you that all these people—more than a couple—are taking advantage of you? They're totally using you for free babysitting."

"I'm fully aware of the situation," she would explain. "But if they're not here, at our home, they're home alone. It's the kid who suffers, not the parent, if I turn the kid away. Besides, I get to spend all this time with these great kids. I'm the lucky one." Not only did she not care what the other parents, or society at large, might think—specifically, that she was weak and foolish—but she did the right thing for a lot of kids who, as you can imagine, still love her.

My mom doesn't expect me to be like her or agree with her on all things, and she certainly isn't threatened by our differences. I don't sew like she did, but I paint, and I make funny faces and make up stories like she did, and so much of how I mother is influenced by her. But we're different, too, and these variations aren't important elements to motherhood. They're individual quirks that are slightly interesting personality traits. For example, my mom irons her sheets and pillowcases. I do not. My mother doesn't do this out of obligation or appearances or for any other reason than that she wants to do it. She likes having ironed sheets. (You should have seen how excited both my mom and dad were when my dad found an old steam press at the thrift store for $75. It was an amazing and completely bizarre sight forever burned in my mind.) My mom's idea of motherhood isn't tied up with housekeeping. She doesn't care if I iron my sheets or not. She never insisted I do it to be a good mother. Mothering means *more* than that. And yet, she doesn't stop doing it, something she personally likes, for fear of being mocked or seen as old-fashioned. She does it anyway. She's awesome.

Modern mothering does not need more advice giving or tests that will, once and for all, give us a definitive answer at who is doing it best. It does need a call to retire the jokes about our jeans. *We get it! Moms used to wear elastic-banded jeans that made their torsos look really nonexistent and their backsides really big. That was funny. Ha ha. It's not **a thing** anymore!*

How do we do "our job"? How do we fully prepare for our children to live and thrive without us? By lowering the bar and . . . just kidding. I'm not giving you advice. I'm not your mom.

Side Rant

Do you know what IS a "thing"? Vinyl lettering on our walls with inspirational quotes, that's a thing we do. Also, Zumba, that's another "thing." Huge packs of moms get together several times a week and attempt Latin and hip-hop dance, some more successfully than others, and wear shredded T-shirts and fluorescent baggy pants and leopard-print high-tops while doing it. That's something to make fun of: Because we actually DO it. Oh, and we LIKE it!

So You've Created Your Birth Plan, Now What?

Or, I don't know how to parent you

Or, All the different phases of parenting are alike
in that they include fear and bliss

It's very popular, and tempting, for first-time moms to spend what I think is a disproportionate amount of time obsessing over how their baby's *birth* should go instead of getting down to issues that will have more impact on their lasting legacy as "mom." Instead of spending so much time talking, and planning, and defending what happens in the ONE DAY, this first day, maybe a prospective mom should spend a bit of that time thinking about what will happen on, say, day 5,864, and start studying calculus so that when her tenth grader is failing it, she'll be able to help him. Just a suggestion.

Power shifts in parenting came to me when I wasn't looking. In a span of four months, I went from having little kids to having two of my kids become taller than me. It's been years since I could help my sons with math (and I took calculus in high school and used to be able to do it), and I can't help my third grader with French. Who am I kidding—I couldn't help him in the first grade. When you cannot help them with their homework and they realize that they have surpassed you in some area, and you see on their face the smug look of satisfaction with a twinge of embarrassment FOR YOU, well, it's, let's say, *different* from planning which music you will listen to while in labor, or which outfit you will dress them in to come home from the hospital. When you offer to help your kids with something, and they don't believe you can—THAT DAY will come, too. (And where are the message boards about THAT?)

When we were expecting our oldest child, in 1998, I decided to take a Lamaze class. My mother was really into Lamaze and natural childbirth and was really good at it. She was so good at it that she taught another mother who was in the bed next to her in the hospital the relaxing and breathing techniques WHILE SHE WAS IN LABOR WITH ME. Talk about multitasking and overachieving (but that's another story). So I thought Lamaze was my legacy.

During the course of the class, however, it became pretty apparent that I didn't have what it takes to fully commit myself to the cause of natural childbirth. I think that became most obvious when we viewed a film showcasing different positions to try during labor. One of the scenes showed a husband and pregnant wife in the shower, hunched over, with the water beating on the wife's back, while the narrator instructed that not only will warm water relax the mother, but also "singing a soothing song." The husband started singing, "She'll be comin' round the mountain when she comes! She'll be . . ." and we lost it. Of ALL the songs! It was the most ridiculous thing I had ever seen. Months later, Topher thought it would be "funny" to start singing "She'll be comin' round the mountain . . ." when I was in full labor. It wasn't funny and I asked for an epidural.

Our Birth Plan:

We want the baby to come out. That's our plan.

I don't mean to minimize the need to be prepared and do your best. The day of your child's birth is overanalyzed for a reason. You're afraid of the unknown, of the pain, or of what *might* happen. You're also excited. You have ideas about what you want it to be like and how you'll feel. It's fear and bliss. Welcome to motherhood. It's more of the same.

Once when I was talking with my oldest son about grades and the reasoning behind my well-intentioned pushing and encouraging, I was smacked in the face with a moment of exasperation. I was desperate. I clearly wasn't communicating with him, so I thought I'd just be simple and honest, and I said, "I don't know how to parent you." He answered, "Yeah, we know." Well, "we know" suggests that not only has Miles identified my inadequacy, but so have the other children, *and they've talked about it.* This is something they've discussed. Bonded over. His reply confirmed my deepest parenting fear.

Coming face-to-face with some of your parenting fears is good because then there's one less thing to fear, right? Choose something else to latch on to and move forward.

Kids are smarter than we think; we can maybe "fake it" with other people, but kids see us at our most vulnerable moments, and they can choose to remember anything they want and form their memories from that (another parenting fear realized). They'll retell the story over and over again of the time you tried to turn off the TV with the home phone. You might have created magical Christmases for eighteen years, but they'll remember the one Christmas you yelled at them to pick up their socks. Yeah, THAT's what they'll remember. Not the hours it took you to make the Christmas casserole or the times you had Topher run to Walgreen's for batteries so Christmas morning wouldn't be ruined, but the time you decided to take a nap when they needed you to do something—like get them a drink. They'll remember the good stuff, too, of course, but memories are dodgy at best. Ask me to recall one distinct memory from the fifth grade. I can't. It's hard. It was a whole year! They all blend together.

Not everyone can be the good mom all the time or sail through every phase of parenting. You may say of someone, "Oh, she's a great mom!" But what you are most likely referring to is her excellence in a particular phase of parenting. (We always judge others' best against our worst, right? As the saying goes. Isn't that a thing? I'm sure I've seen that quote pinned on Pinterest and passed around between guilt-prone moms like myself.) For starters, a lot of people are tripped up by the newborn thing. My friend Rebecca says, "Give me a one-year-old, and I'm good." She's got the toddler phase down. Newborns are hard for her, with the crying and feeding and helplessness. But for others, that's the dream—the smells, the euphoria of falling in love with a new person, the little booties—not hard. But the decision to have a baby is the choice to have a toddler, too. Toddlers with their running around knocking into everything and their sticky messes everywhere and the obstinance. But the chubby fingers and the unrestrained hugs and kisses and the discoveries of every little thing! And small children, and school and systems and routines and questions and negotiating and smelling—well—not like newborns. And preteens and mean girls and risk taking and music lessons (all of these things can be both good and bad) and teenagers and young adults and so on. We all have our favorite stages, and we can't all be good at all of them. But the hope is that they are *phases,* so, by definition, they don't last forever—which is a statement full of both sadness and relief.

I have identified some **parenting stages** I have personally experienced, and a couple I conjured up because I'm not quite there yet.

There's the **ignorant bliss** stage, when you convince yourself that you won't be faced with the kinds of dilemmas you've seen others struggle with. YOU will be different. You won't experience sleeplessness, colic, cradle cap, and the like. Then there's denial, where you really believe that making a detailed birthing plan will fully prepare you for the miracle of birth. Like making a list and reading the texts and taking the classes means "you're doing it right."

Your checklist is carved in stone and you have control. (I miss this phase.)

Then there's the **adjustment** phase, when you realize that you're really tired (maybe I should call this the tired phase) and you're bitter when you see people dressed, knowing they've had a shower and don't constantly smell like spit-up or sour milk. You start counting how many diapers you change in one day and multiply that number by seven, then that number by fifty-two, and that number by two or three, and you feel a little exasperated. You cope. Hopefully you find a good friend in the same stage. That makes it easier. You can hate all the "regular people who don't know how easy their lives are" together. Maybe you start drinking Diet Dr. Pepper or taking a nap for date night. I don't judge anyone in this phase. It's an adjustment.

Then there's the **I got this!** phase, where you've learned a trick or two. You've logged a couple of days of sleeping more than six hours and you feel optimistic. You've got a system and it's working. Bring on the chore charts and the job wheels! This is a great phase. A lot of people start talking about "the next baby" without crying during this phase.

Then there's the **What am I doing?** phase, where you question your policies. You can do that now because things are working, so now you must make life harder for yourself. You're drunk on the power of sleeping more, successfully raising children who are regularly bathed and fed, and it feels good. You're showering now and getting out; you're queen of the world. You start to read blogs and think about homeschooling, stockpiling freezer meals, and considering your Elf on the Shelf policies. This is an overwhelming phase. There are many voices willing to lead you to "motherhood specialization." You start to consider your legacy: are you the "Scouting mom" or the "crafty mom" or the "carefree traveling mom" or the "free range mom"? These are all things. Choose wisely. This phase runs concurrently with the:

Systems phase, where you organize your systems for storing homework, photos, records, and those freezer meals you plan to make once you buy that extra freezer. My friend Kacy has never left and will never leave this phase because of her love of office supplies, particularly binders. This is a fun stage full of design ideas and has kept Target in business for years. Now you're ready to explore extracurricular activities for the kids: dance, soccer, tumbling, musical theater, baseball, chess, art—there are endless options. You start to think, "What if my kid was meant to be an Olympic athlete?" You consider what that might take.

The next phase is the **You're ruining my life!** stage, or the **Busted!** phase, when your kids figure out you don't really know what you're doing. Before, they trusted you completely while you lay in bed stewing over whether you should bribe them for good grades or just expect them. Elf on the Shelf is the least of your problems because now your kids know they have some wiggle room when it comes to your sleepover or technology policies. Everything is up for grabs. It helps to have a friend in this phase at the same time to talk things through. This is where you have to, for your sanity, simplify your policies and stick to the basics. Cereal for dinner doesn't matter. Whether you let your kids have cell phones or Internet on their cell phones is what's on the table now. You can choose two, maybe three things to enforce. Again, choose wisely. I chose church, education, and music. So far I have no regrets, but I don't have an Eagle Scout yet and I'm regularly having the "Your parents were English majors and you're failing ENGLISH!?" discussion with our oldest son. Rome wasn't built in a day.

The next phase is the **acceptance** phase. I'm entering this phase, and it's calm, but eerily so. It's when you realize that you could be the best parent in the world but your kid could still choose to do anything in the world, good or bad. He could be president of a corporation, start a nonprofit that saves children, or drop out of college and sell drugs. Some of my parenting heroes have kids who are turning out well and kids who are ruining their own lives. This is a heartbreaking phase. When your kids are younger, it's easy to convince yourself that they will choose to do what you say or want them to do because they want to please you, for the most part. It's easy to believe, when they're little, that you are the exception; you can quiet the voice that says they have the power to break your heart. This is the phase when you realize that you love them even more than you did when they were babies (a concept you couldn't have imagined at the time) because they're "real people" now and you like them. The stakes are high, and they have all the power. In previous stages I would hear the advice, "Just love them," and think, "Yeah, yeah, of course, but what else? Don't let them sleep over at their friends' houses and limit video games to the weekends after chores, right? Right?!" I wanted a checklist to somehow guarantee the best outcome, but a list alone can never do that. What's really important are the feelings behind the rules and boundaries we set. So now I think, "Oh. Just love them. Got it."

The final stage that I've identified (I'm not there yet, so this is all conjecture) is the **mysterious older lady** phase, for lack of a better title. (It's a working title actually, I just really like mysterious older ladies. I'm not joking.) This is the phase when you have a lot of the answers, when your heart has been broken (usually by your kids, sometimes by your spouse or just by life), and you know things. Deep things. This is the phase when you're qualified to give advice, but no one thinks you really have any. Because times have changed and you didn't have email in college or blogs when you were a young mom, people think your advice is outdated. But these mysterious women know and have it figured out and they are who I want to sit next to. This stage is when you have had to "just love them" because there was no other choice, and you and they have lived through it.

The ebb and flow in and out of the different stages of life is interesting to me. I'm not good with change, particularly transitions. I'm the sort of mother who will close my eyes and *will* time to stop because THIS is the best stage of life for my family, when they're like THIS. I check in on them sleeping in their beds and cry over them, anticipating the day when we won't be sleeping under the same roof every night. (I'm getting teary about this now because, as established earlier, I clearly have issues.) I'm interested in being effective and avoiding as much pain as possible. I don't think there would be anything more painful in the fight to raise my kids than "what-if-ing" myself to death, wishing I'd done more or done it better or *(cold panic)* completely differently. In each stage I think: *How can I be the most effective mom? What is the best I can offer my kids? What parenting practices actually work?* Crying over the children while they sleep is clearly not an effective parenting strategy, but it's a good coping skill.

I'm going to be an overconfident grandma for sure.

The Anatomy of a Playdate

My friend Josh called me the other day, and this was our conversation:

Josh: Hello, Lisa!
Lisa: Hey! How are you?
Josh: Great! Can Seth come over tomorrow from 2 to 3:30?
Lisa: Yeah, that time works great for us. Hugh will be so excited!
Josh: Great! Thanks, and see you tomorrow!

scene (approximately 14 seconds)

I got off the phone and laughed—absolutely delighted. This is how 99 percent of my playdate conversations typically go:

Judy: Hello, Lisa!
Lisa: Oh, hi, Judy!
Judy: How are you?
Lisa: Good! How are you?
Judy: Oh, great! You doin' okay, then? Topher gone a lot?
Lisa: Yeah, his play is [over/winding down/in the middle of rehearsals/whatever]; you should go see it!
Judy: Yeah, I will, I will. . . .
Lisa: What's going on with you guys? You all right?
Judy: Yeah, things are going well for us . . . [insert report on each member of the family]. What about you guys?
Lisa: [Insert report on each member of the family. Add one cute story.]
Judy: [Laughs. Comments on story, like, "Oh, that's our Hugh!" or, "Oh, if I had a NICKEL!"]
pause
Lisa: Well, what can I do for you?
Judy: Well, I hesitate to ask . . . I know you're so busy!

Lisa: Well, you are TOO! What are you talking about!?

Judy: Well, what are you doing on Friday?

Lisa: Oh, [insert some joke about a menial household task, most likely laundry, or an exasperated expression, like, "just trying to hold it together!" or, "just wrangling the monkeys!"]

Judy: Yeah, tell me about it!

pause

Judy: Well, AND YOU CAN SAY NO, but, is there ANY way Trevor could come over on Friday for a couple of hours while I [insert task that could be considered fun, but make it sound necessary and something you can't get out of] . . . ?

Lisa: Well, sure! I'm sure Trevor and Hugh will have a great time! It will be fun!

Judy: Are you SURE? And, you know, I'll return the favor! Anytime, anytime!

Lisa: Oh, I know! I'll be sure to take you up on that!

Judy: Do! Do!

Lisa: I will! [maybe]

Judy: I'm going to hold you to that!

Lisa: Okay.

Judy: Well, if something comes up, let me know.

Lisa: I will. I'll see you Friday!

Judy: Okay! And thanks a lot. I'll see you Friday. And, one of these days, we need to get together and go to lunch! We just need to DO IT!

Lisa: I know, right?

Judy: Okay. Talk to you soon!

Lisa: 'Bye!

Judy: 'Bye!

scene (approximately 24 minutes)

Come Sundown, We'll Put On a Show!

Or, Every woman has something different to offer

In the impending apocalypse, we're all going to need to band together in order to survive. Our individual skills will be used for the common good and justify our place within the pack. Our skill could mean the difference between life and death. In our small communities, as we wander looking for shelter, maybe hiding out in the mountains, maybe running from zombies (who can say for sure?), what will your contribution be? Are you good with weapons? Can you fix cars, rework plumbing, or dig latrines? Build homes? Plant and harvest food? This was the gist of some comments my husband and I heard in Sunday School class (minus the zombie part, which I added for emphasis) soon after moving to the small seaside town of Dawlish, England, so that he could begin work on a master's degree in Staging Shakespeare.

My husband and I are good at none of those things that were listed in Sunday School that day. We were there to develop Christopher's specific talent—Shakespeare and directing—while I was writing and reading but mostly caring for small children. Basically, we're theater nerds. Initially deflated, we thought on it and decided that the things we are good at might not "save lives" or "be needed," but they will certainly distract us from our troubles and rouse our spirits, which is not insignificant when you're rationing your #10 cans of hard wheat and identifying edible bugs along the road. For a can of beans, a bottle of sterile alcohol, and half a pack of Band-Aids, come sundown, we'll put on a show!

That was not the first time I've had to carefully consider what I have to contribute to the world. My mother and my two sisters are all really great seamstresses. My dear mother tried to teach me to sew. There was an unfortunate incident when I was a teenager with a peach knit "units" outfit (*remember that store in the mall from the '80s? They sold tubes of stretch fabric in every color and each piece could be a top or a skirt or a belt and you could mix and match? My super-cool cousin Julie worked there and it was totally rad*) and some frustration with threading the machine, and things were said . . . and I used to feel like such a failure at this skill that I thought was my birthright. Add to that the fact that my mother sewed my (modest) prom dresses; my sister Gina has a small business making custom drapery, bedding, and clothes; and my other sister, Amanda, is a famous fashion designer who appeared on the eleventh and thirteenth seasons of the reality TV show *Project Runway*. Yeah.

But being pushed to the edge of humiliating failure made me realize that I'm good at other things—like making videos on the Internet like a fourteen-year-old boy. And I'll take it. I used to think that I had to fit the Relief Society mold and to meet all the needs that someone else was expecting of me instead of being careful and deliberate but generous with my own offering. That mind-set was not helpful. Those kinds of self-doubt keep people, particularly women, from creating and living authentic, deliberate lives in which we make choices based on what WE want and on what WE like.

As women, I think one of our most often overlooked strengths is found in our differences. We all offer something different as individuals, as well as in our communities. In the gospel sense, we each have a gift to contribute, an "offering." We learn in the scriptures about the body of Christ, how each element is essential and serves the common good (see 1 Corinthians 12:14–27). We teach our children that being different is good. We want variety in everything from our entertainment to our food and educational choices. But do we enthusiastically encourage each other to be who we really are—which is different from each other?

For example, I love improvisational acting. I love going on stage not knowing who I'll be or what I'll say and contributing to a scene and being creative. What I've found that I like to do—what my passion is—is unusual. We don't have Relief Society mini classes on improv. It's a specialized offering. I try to find opportunities to serve in this way, however, that meet my ward's needs, or my family's, and I have used this skill many times in those settings. I really have. Some people might think that's silly. I'm not curing cancer, it's true. But it's something. It brings me so much joy and personal satisfaction—and it's my offering. I haven't always thought this way, but I have (mostly) quit trying to compare my gift with others' offerings that I think are more significant because that's immobilizing and unproductive.

We need to know what we like (and what we don't like) and make conscious, well-thought-out, deliberate decisions about what kind of life we want to lead. We can't get caught up in what others expect from us and what we think we have to do. We need to own our own decisions. This involves a lot of time, prayer, self-reflection, and, I think, humility, because sometimes what we like isn't cool or convenient. And a lot of the time it means disappointing someone else's expectation of us, someone we really care about. Plus, as moms, we often have to set aside our own needs to care for others, and under those circumstances it's easy to get lost and forget what we like. Or sometimes what we like even changes over time, but we get so busy we fail to recognize that. Ultimately, who we decide to be is up to us. And our "offerings" to the Church, to our families, and to the world are twisted up in who we are.

My friend Hailey is an exceptional actor and singer. I know I will embarrass her by stating that she could star in a Broadway show right now and hold her own, but it's true. She is the mom of four, and as much as she loves being the dramatic song leader at church, she needs more. She craves regular opportunities, big and small, to be creative, whether it's singing, acting, writing, or (mostly) performing. A lot of people don't understand why she needs to take time away from family or work to do these things. She explains: "I'm a better mom and a happier person when I know I have a performance or creative project coming up. I don't know why this is, but it just is. I'm happier, I'm more patient with my kids, I'm a more fun mom. I need it, and everyone's happier!" It's weird for me to think, "Well, why do you need to get on stage and act out a story about garlic toast and space aliens?" (remember, improv relies on suggestions from the audience), but I get it. A creative project helps to energize your whole life. I don't understand why my friend Kacy feels the need to volunteer to foster stray cats and dogs (I wasn't born with the "loving animals" gene), but it sustains her in a real way as well.

My family is a good example of this concept of finding your individual offerings because we all do different, really specific things for a living. My parents were really great about not living through us but rather encouraging us to make our own decisions and deluding us into thinking we could do or be anything we wanted to as long as we worked hard. It wasn't until we were older that we realized that time, money, circumstance, and outside forces could stop us from achieving what we wanted. But by that time it was too late. So my oldest brother, Christopher, is a doctor in family practice who is a painter on the side; I'm a Super Mormony Mom (I go to all three hours of church every Sunday and everything) and I write and act; my sister Gina is also a Super Mormony Mom who sews and runs marathons; my little brother, James, is the lead guitarist for Maroon5 (do you like how I snuck that in? A literal rock star); and my youngest sister, Amanda, is a well-known stylist and Nashville fashion designer. And maybe it's the "Super Mormony Mom" title going to my head (I don't mean to brag), but we are more than what we do for a living. I only mention it to illustrate that I literally know what it feels like to be UNCOOL and take a gooood long look at your life's decisions and question everything. I know what it feels like to be eight months pregnant at home with toddlers all day, cleaning red-Kool-Aid-induced vomit off of the carpet, silently chastising yourself for offering your son RED KOOL-AID when he told you he wasn't feeling that great, when your rock-star brother calls from the Grammys after having just won. AGAIN. I know what it feels like to feel pretty good about yourself for potty-training your kid, to share it with your family, only to hear about your other brother who snatched an infant from the jaws of death with a life-saving technique. I understand comparing each other's gifts.

But do we get so caught up in comparing that we forget to be *grateful* for each other's offerings, for the sum of all the parts? We need to honor our own gifts and allow others, even encourage others, to have their own. There's not a limited number of pie pieces. Someone else's success is not our failure. We can't all be the same. It doesn't work.

In parenting and in our daily interactions with others, we are constantly evaluating our own performance as Christians. Self-evaluation is necessary to check ourselves: Are we on the right path? Are our hearts in the right place? Combine that with mothering and the self-evaluation *that* requires, and there's a lot of judgment. It's hard to switch that off. I think one of the reasons why women, and particularly women in the Church, are so hard on themselves is because of out-of-control judgment. We forget mercy and grace, and because we want to get everything done, and because what we do matters, we want to "clean up" everything around us.

In discussing how women judge each other, my sister Gina cryptically said, "Sometimes the hardest sister you learn to love is your own." I'm not sure what she meant by that, but I do know that she and I tease each other about competing to be the best mom. We like to one-up each other, like, "I'll see your homemade baby food and I'll raise you piano lessons," or, "I'll see your reading to your kids every night and raise you hand-sewn Easter dresses," and so on. I have five children. They were all born in the hospital, and I had an epidural with every one of them. That's something that I don't have conflicting feelings about, although I know some women do. Our mother had five children using Lamaze and no drugs, and she is the best mom we know. So when Gina announced she might try natural childbirth, she wanted to use it like she uses marathon running—as a way to show me that she is physically stronger than I am (which she is) and a way to be more like Mom (my Kryptonite! We both want to be like Mom!). So it became our funny competition, with her bragging that she was physically and mentally strong enough to do it when I wasn't, and me pretending I didn't care, telling her it wasn't that big of a deal. I reminded her that you don't get a medal or anything if you don't have an epidural. You get a baby—that's the prize. We all get the same prize!

Fast-forward to the day of her daughter's birth, and the choice that we had stood on opposite sides of came—and, interestingly enough, the choice was taken away from her. The anesthesiologist didn't show up. He was called away on an emergency, and Gina *had to* have natural childbirth. When I went to see her in the hospital, I brought her a homemade medal made from a Mason-jar lid covered in tinfoil with "#1 MOM!" written in Sharpie, with a red ribbon so she could wear it around her neck. She had won. I relented. She loved the medal and wore it in the hospital while I held my new niece. Then she said that of course natural childbirth was totally awesome and such a rush, and laughingly admitted she probably wouldn't do that again. But then she did (show-off).

Gina and I can agree or disagree and laugh at each other, but I wouldn't make a medal like that for just anyone. I did it because I knew she would think it was funny. I admit that I have a hard time relating to women who take themselves too seriously. I think we miss the lessons in life when we miss the humor, and because I feel strongly about that, it's difficult for me to suspend judgment. But I know that my way of seeing the world isn't necessarily right, and I know I say a lot of dumb things and need people to constantly give me the benefit of the doubt, so I'm working on doing that for others.

Do you get the sense that some people cut themselves off from different kinds of moms out of a fear that those moms' experiences somehow devalue their own? That's not true. I can be grateful for my own life choices, the ones that brought me to where I am and helped make me who I am, and still learn and find significant value in others' choices. Valuing others' choices doesn't mean I'm turning my back on my personal choices or crumbling or feeling inadequate (which is easy to do). There are great benefits in really getting to know our differences: We can gain ideas of how to improve our own and our kids' lives. Our capacity to love increases as we feel increased sympathy toward others and compassion for situations we hadn't realized existed. We can grow in gratitude for our own situation. Our eyes are opened to more opportunities. And we come to recognize assumptions we have made about ourselves, our families, and our communities that we didn't even know we held. Seeing through different eyes the ideas we have attached to our marriage, family, religion, culture, and identity allows us to "clean house" and get to the truth.

I think in order to relate to each other amid differences large and small, we need to not downplay our differences but celebrate them. We need to ask: "What have you learned? What has surprised you about your life? What do you wish you had known ten years ago?" and other open-ended questions. We can change the tone of the conversation. Asking questions with the belief that the other has something important to say as a woman, as a mother, as a sister in the gospel, or as a neighbor indicates your openness to engage in a real conversation. We can't have a tone of "either/or" or "us/them." We can't ask with accusing insinuations like "How can you live the gospel and . . . (vote this way, have that job, wear that, do this, feel that)?" We need to just listen.

Seeing differences in each other helps us not trap others, or get trapped ourselves, in stereotypes. Being seen as an individual is religiously and personally significant. But sometimes we get caught up in "motherhood specialization," seeking to validate our choice in some area of mothering that we feel confident in: *"I'm the (fill-in-the-blank) mom."* The media repeatedly refers to this phenomenon under the heading of "Mommy Wars," all of which I think is ridiculous and not helpful. No one offers any real solutions to real-world challenges because the point is to take sides, so everyone lines up ready to fight, which is not going to change anyone's mind. Everyone's just trying to prove their own point and BE right rather than to learn from one another.

We are all the exception. Our kids are all different, and when we have respect for others' choices and lifestyles, it gives us confidence to have more respect for our own choices. It helps us maintain our focus in mothering. It frees us up to ask "Am I doing the best for me and my kids?" rather than "How will others view this choice?" Our respect builds other moms up. We can't empathize in all things because we all have limited experiences. We all have regrets, triumphs, success, hardship. I hear about someone performing all over the world or going to grad school, and there's a twinge, a whisper that I have missed out. But then I remember that I have traveled, I have five amazing kids, and I've had lots of other great experiences. Each of us only gets one lifetime. We're all limited in some ways and blessed in others.

It's good, of course, to sometimes reexamine our own choices and reevaluate our decisions and make changes if necessary. In fact, I'm pretty sure it's required of those who want to live a Christlike

Side Rant

One of the most divisive battles in the "Mommy Wars" is between the SAHMs vs. the working moms. That's really funny to me because what is "staying at home" vs. "working" anyway? What constitutes "working"? How much you accomplish or how much you invoice? Full-time? Part-time? Ten hours a week or more?. Do you have to be receiving benefits or have an official W-2? Does the type or quality of work influence the judgment? Or salary or needs of the family? Does it have to be paid work, or does volunteering count? Does it have to be a sacrifice? Does your desire to be on the other side of the argument include you on both sides? Is it more honorable if you say you wish you worked or wish you could stay at home? It's ridiculous. They're BOTH HARD and ridden with challenges. Now what?

life. The "Maybe I should have" and "Maybe I shouldn't have's" can disarm heated moments, generate better ideas, foster openmindedness, and create a less-threatened way of life. "It's a possibility . . ." and other statements of tentativeness are not the end of personal identity. We're so used to saying we know "without a shadow of a doubt" the truth of many elements in our faith. Why can't we make more statements *with* a shadow of a doubt in other aspects of our lives? Is that really so horrible? Won't it actually reduce the number of truths we *really* know and thereby concentrate their emphasis and importance?

But while we need to be open to new possibilities, ultimately we become our own kind of mom when we *own* our choices. We know we can't choose all of the good things we want to do, but we've made some specific choices, and we can live with that. We feel confident in who we are, but we know that we are not just "who we are." We see life as a process; we're always evolving, we're on a journey, we're going in a direction. We've made some mistakes, but that helps us understand the Atonement better because forgiveness is a big part of our life. And what the Atonement means to ourselves and to others—how we access it, feel it, offer it, embrace it—becomes something real because we have to constantly practice it. We see that we have power to make life, and ourselves, better. And we respect that others do, too.

It makes me sad when mothers are unkind to themselves while serving and loving others with such capability and in such abundance. We need to be gentle with ourselves. One thing that we never have to worry about is creating conflict for others in order to "teach them how life really is." Life will do that enough for them and for all of us. We don't need to pretend that some people just don't have to deal with the kinds of trials we've had, or that if they did, they endured them better than we ever could. Elder Neal Maxwell illustrated this when he wrote:

"We must be careful . . . not to canonize [our role] models as we have some pioneers and past Church leaders—not to dry all the human sweat off them, not to put ceaseless smiles on their faces, when they really struggled and experienced agony. Real people who believe and prevail are ultimately more faith-promoting and impressive than saccharine saints with tinsel traits."

We need each other, and we need to teach of Christ and do what He would have us do, which is often contrary to what we would naturally choose to do. It's harder, and it's messy and sweaty, but that's what we're trying to do as a body of imperfect Saints.

If I could have my one "sit down and buy the world a Coke moment," I would want to tell everyone that no woman is defined by one incident in her life, one job, one career, one zip code, one choice. We don't know all the information, but we can each seek the Spirit to find the best ways we can contribute. And we can be more kind, especially when we're talking about how we see the world and ourselves—even when our perspectives are different, as they most likely will be. It would be great if we as women could lead the way and form a real sisterhood: friends who give each other the benefit of the doubt. The stakes are high in what we're asked to do in raising human beings; wouldn't it be great if we felt that everyone was on our side?

What to Say to a Pregnant Woman

1. Would you like to sit down?

2. You look beautiful.

3. Would you like a cookie? *(Thank you, Emmie!)*

4. (optional) What KIND of cookie would you like? *Warning: Before asking this question, make sure there actually is a variety of cookies to offer. Don't mess around making empty promises.

   You will be tempted to say more. You think you are clever and charming. In this case, you are not. Know your audience. You may not know what to say, and if you let your nervousness get the best of you, you'll say something inappropriate even though you "mean well." IT'S NOT WORTH IT. Unless she's told you there is more than one baby in there, there is not. She will, indeed, never "pop" (that's not a thing), and she is constantly aware of how much time she has "left." Get comfortable with sitting in uncomfortable silence. It's okay.

I'm the One in the Dented Minivan

Or, Livin' on the edge

Or, Motherhood is like a lot of things,
but unlike anything else

I sometimes forget that the make, model, and condition of my car does not indicate who I am—who I *really* am. Well, that's not entirely true. I actually love the dent on the driver's side of the minivan because it reminds me of how much I live on the edge.

One 24th of July we were visiting some friends when their neighbors brought over some serious fireworks. As we "oooed!" and "ahhhhed!," all looking straight up in the air, mouths agape, unbeknownst to us, the firework package had tipped over and was pointed straight at us all. A neighbor ran to tip the firework back into its upright position just in time for the next round to go off and run up his cheek, dangerously near his eye. We saw him place the package upright on the ground, then watched it knock itself over again and shoot the next round right across the street, into my van door. I love that dent. It means the children are safe and we made a good story together. Later that evening, the neighbor brought over custom lemon custard as we all re-told his feat of *"literally* saving our lives and risking his eye" in the process, and we imagined in detail, with "tsks!" and "wows!," what would have happened if the fireworks had shot into the crowd: *"The children!"* we exclaimed in excited tones and moved our heads side to side. Yes, a hero and a family tale were born that night. And the dent remains.

But I also have a second, mysterious dent of unknown origins. I don't love that dent. It reminds me that someone hit my car and didn't leave a note. You win some, you lose some.

My minivan is also a litmus test in problem solving, so I feel like I'm really giving my kids an advantage for the future in that regard. It amazes me that most kids today truly don't know how to open up a van door. This happens 100 percent of the time anyone under the age of twenty-one comes into my 2000 Dodge Grand Caravan: They stand in front of the door, waiting for it to open automatically. It doesn't. This car was built before most of them were born. I yell, "You have to open the door! It's not one of those that open . . . you're just going to have to slide it . . . yank it open!" At this point they look confused and inevitably shrug, presumably looking for a doorknob/handle/lever, and about 23 percent of them locate it, but of those 23 percent, none of them can successfully operate it to open the door. Not one. It's the weirdest phenomenon. (Has our reliance on technology atrophied our arm muscles already? Are we living in the future NOW?) They yank. They look confused, and, preemptively, while my own kids have been staring at the door or looking aimlessly around at no one in particular, I've been telling them, "Just do it. Just open the door. Just . . ." and soon my kids are telling their friends (like it's obvious), "JUST PUSH THE BUTTON AND SLIDE THE DOOR OPEN!" Twelve percent of that group is able to, and I usually sigh at this point. (My youngest, Margaret, always asks me why I sigh so loud. I tell her I'm just trying to catch my breath. Which I am. I'm also reevaluating the choices that brought me to this point. This "point of SIGH.")

I sigh and say, "You have to yank it really hard! We spilled some root beer in the track and it sticks . . ." I trail off here because I know I should just get out of the car, walk around to the passenger's side, and open the door myself, and we could avoid all of these embarrassing apologies in my head, but when I consider doing that—GETTING OUT OF THE CAR (which is

Side Rant

Like I owe somebody else's kids an explanation about why that thirty-two-ounce root beer spilled all over the door track and why I wasn't able to clean it up in a timely manner! And why I haven't been able to clean it up in an untimely manner. I mean, I'm giving them a ride somewhere, for goodness' sake! I don't have to explain why the door doesn't magically open for them. I want to scream, "Expectations are the root of heartache!" But then I'll just be the crazy lady who screams Shakespeare quotes at them, and I'm already the crazy lady whose van door doesn't open up and who sighs repeatedly.

the worst thing in the world, the crowning symbol of inconvenience)—I get indignant.

Ultimately, they either yank the handle to the side and the door opens (5 percent of the time) or one of my kids opens it. And that's what technology is doing to our kids: They can't OPEN DOORS, PEOPLE! And then, 98 percent of the time, my kids say something like "When are we getting a new car?" and I catch my breath. Really loudly.

It's not like I don't dream of or imagine better cars, a better home, a more glamorous life. It's just that I've relegated that creative dreaming to the spot where it is most useful: the imaginary world of Pinterest. Don't mistake me: I think Pinterest is a great organizer of ideas, and it has allowed me to throw away all those glossy *Modern Living* magazine pages I had stored in files for "someday," but sometimes I have to take a time-out from it. Sometimes the collecting, the pinning, and the creating of creative boards becomes the creative outlet and not the inspiration for an actual, real-life creative outlet. Also, thanks to Pinterest, now I want a two-story loft treehouse made out of books that spell out "READ!," and I'd like it to be lit by magical Mason-jar lights that require no electricity while I'm eating a cheesecake that has a brownie crust and Reese's Peanut Butter Cups baked in the center—but I just have to live in a world where that's probably not going to happen for me. (Truth be told, I'll probably try the cheesecake recipe.) I just need to balance my personal goals and dreams in a real-world setting without losing hope and throwing out

Pinterest completely. Without it, how would I feed my obsession for the idea of (not the execution of) freezer meals and get new ideas for Primary music time?

But I've made my choices. And I own them. Of course, that's easy to say when things are running relatively smoothly. When your kids are all snug in their beds dreaming away, the kitchen is clean, the floors are clear of dirty socks and random bits of paper, and all you can hear is the gentle hum of the dishwasher, it's easy to be satisfied that everything's all right and you're on top of it all. It's when you find your basement flooding, or discover your kid isn't turning in school assignments, or realize you've missed a work deadline—that's when you begin to worry that everything is falling apart, or could at a moment's notice, like that critical block in the middle of the Jenga game that brings everything crashing down.

It is often said that motherhood is a lot of things: a roller coaster, a bad boyfriend, a carnival, a marathon, a horror movie, whatever, but really motherhood is unlike anything else. And I'm not even trying to say that it's like a dented minivan (although if this were a question on the ACT, minivans to mothers is like space shuttle to astronaut) because that comparison doesn't fully capture it all either. I mean, I like the analogy in the sense that we're on a journey together, there's room for everyone, and it's messy but fun. But the van metaphor for motherhood could go the other way, too: it's just to get from point A to point B, it breaks down a lot, it depreciates in value (see, not a great comparison—pretty flawed, actually).

Motherhood defies analogy and categorization because as prepared as we think we are, as motivated, well-intentioned, and dedicated, we never seem to be the kind of mother we set out to be. That can be both good and bad. Motherhood changes us. It has us constantly adjusting for the unexpected. And it has a way of revealing the best and worst in us, which is a beautiful, humiliating way of life. Living on the edge.

Why Are Leaving Dirty Dishes in the Sink and Keeping the Cobwebs Intact a Prerequisite to "Enjoying Your Kids"?

Or, You can have a clean house and enjoy your kids' childhood at the same time!

Or, Lower the stakes: housework and mothering are different things

I come from a long line of clean ~~freaks~~ people. My mother made cleaning look effortless, although we all know it's not. She just didn't complain about it; she was really productive. A lot of my memories of talking with her involve her simultaneously doing something else: folding laundry, making dinner, cleaning up, picking up. She insisted that we work too, and she told us clearly what she expected us to do. "It's just how Valentines live," my parents would say. "We don't live with a lot of junk around or in a mess. Work hard, then play hard."

My dad takes cleaning to a new level, however. He has a vacuum to clean his vacuum. (That's not a hyperbole for a joke's sake. That's just a fact.) He has a 7-step garbage system. (If I had made that up, why would I choose the number 7? I would choose something more believable like 3, or something ridiculous like 10.) My brother Chris gave him a handheld Dyson vacuum for Christmas one year, and I think my dad cried a little. If I ever want to taunt my father, I just tell him I'm bringing the grandkids over and I'm handing them a bag of crushed potato chips and Fudgesicles before I send them inside. That's how I was taken out of the will.

I don't think you *have* to have a clean, organized home to be a good mom. My feelings about parenting aren't totally enmeshed with housework. I think this is partly because my mom didn't make a big deal about cleaning when I was younger but still made us do it, and partly because I know a lot of excellent moms who have messy homes, and partly because my father is ~~OCD~~ passionate about cleanliness and loves to clean, so I don't identify it as being exclusively a "mom" thing.

Having said that, I do love a clean home. It doesn't mean I love cleaning, but I do find myself sounding a lot like my dad as I wander around the house wiping things down with a soapy rag and mumbling, "Why is everything so sticky? Just wash your hands . . . sheesh! We don't live like this!"

So I resent the little rhymes that say something to the effect of, "Hey, dust and cobwebs, don't bother me right now because I'm spending these precious moments with my baby, who won't be little for long." Which I read as: "Let your house go and sit and stare at your baby. If you feel like cleaning, don't do it, or your baby will grow up FASTER. Or, if you don't feel like cleaning, even better, because it means you're enjoying your kids more." Or something like that. First of all, it's really offensive to a sen-timental, heart-on-her-sleeve mother to be reminded that her kids are growing up. I try to think of ways to stop time or slow it down because I want my kids to stay with me like this forever. I already know that's not going to happen, so keep the advice on the inevitability of time marching on to yourself! (Admittedly, I may be reading too much into this poem.)

The reason I think a clean home is so impor-tant, whether you love cleaning it or not, is because it's setting the stage for how your kids see the world. My phi-losophy is that our homes should be as much as possible like the world should be (not the way it is). It should be organized, simple, clean, and peaceful. Cleaning doesn't have to mean more than that.

Side Rant

If it's so horrible that our children are going to leave us one day to live lives of their own (which is wonderful, too), shouldn't we console ourselves by focusing on the silver linings when possible? I WILL miss messy kisses and spontaneous, unso-licited, unrestrained hugs that knock you over, but I'm not going to miss stepping on Legos, wiping the refrigerator handles a million times a day, or finding candy wrappers all over my house. When my little ones leave me, can't I find a little solace and comfort in not having to wipe a big mess off the toilet seat or change the fitted sheet on the top bunk? I have to miss those things, too?

We mix up housework with motherhood, which is weird. But we do. Here's an excerpt from my journal in 2010 that illustrates what I mean:

I know raising children will pay off to those who matter most to me in the most significant ways, of course, or I wouldn't be doing it. . . . And in those moments, like today, when I'm vacuuming up tortilla chips from under the area rugs for the second time of the day, or wiping bubblegum shake off the walls from three days ago, and I think about how I was a "featured extra" in a movie, but just got a call telling me my scene found its way on the cutting-room floor, I look at my beautiful son Hugh and my adorable toddler Margaret drawing with marker on the family room couch, and I smile, drinking it all in, and I know it's all worth it.

*Just kidding! I tell them **to knock it off**, that we don't draw on the furniture forcryingoutloud, and I clean it up and weep softly. It's worth it, my beautiful darlings, but my parenting skill isn't directly proportional to my ability to clean FORCRYINGOUTLOUD!*

Of course I understand that the meaning of those rhyming poems is to tell mothers to relax about the clean-house thing when they're overwhelmed with the raising-human-beings thing. I get it: Live in the moment. Don't be so rushed that you miss opportunities to read with your children, or sing, or rock them, or play, or make memories. Don't be so obsessed with cleaning that you're not obsessed with your baby. Of course. I just think the poem illustrates an antiquated, sexist idea that the mom is in charge of all the cleaning. I can hear my mother's voice: "Let's just pick up all the toys really quick! Five minutes max." And I can close my eyes and see my dad cleaning the kitchen and insisting, "Doesn't it feel better to live in a clean house? Now we can think!" This is a group effort.

I realize that this is a hot topic among mothers, and I know there are a lot of feelings behind cleaning and who should do it and how it should be done and what it all means. I know that I'm going dangerously near the waters of advice with this chapter, but I am Robert Valentine's daughter, and he would tell me to say, "Just clean your house. Throw half of your stuff away. Stop living with junk! Everyone collects JUNK we don't need!" And perhaps I should just write a manifesto for the clean house and be on my way, but I do think families could all benefit from lowering the stakes on what cleaning means.

For example, I think that a lot of people spend more time *thinking* about making the bed than the amount of time it actually takes to make the bed. Sincerely, you can make a bed in thirty seconds if you focus. Time yourself if you need to. Or, if you really need motivation to clean, just do what I do and watch an episode of *Hoarders* and clean the bathroom during the commercial breaks. That'll give you some motivation. When everything is in order and has a place, it saves time and frustration. I think that having less stuff is the cheater's guide to cleaning, and I'm for it. I'm a "living-with-less-stuff, everyone-lives-in-this-house-so-everyone-cleans, it's-no-big-deal-just-do-it-really-quick, I'll-check-to-see-if-you-did-it-so-just-do-it, no-seriously-this-is-how-we-are-living, we're-all-doing-it" kind of mom.

I like it when I consider that I'm sending children out into the world who know how to clean a bathroom or how to really scrub a kitchen. It's a gift to the world, isn't it? Because YES, I KNOW THEY GROW UP, and by then all I'll have to keep me company are those dusty cobwebs. Well, not really, because I'll have cleaned them up, so then what will I have? If I'm lucky, I'll have my very own garbage system and several vacuums of varying sizes.

What to Say to a Mother of Toddlers

1. You are amazing, and what you do is akin to what is asked of terrorist negotiators.

2. Hairspray gets out ink, and once I got Sharpie out with a Magic Eraser.

3. Would you like to take a nap while I take your child for a few hours?

Making It All Up: How Improvisation Taught Me How to Be a Mom

Or, Moms: managers of the unexpected because we all know Plan A rarely seems to see the light of day

I love improvisational acting. I love going on stage not knowing what character I'll be or what I'll say and contributing to a scene and ultimately a story with a group of talented friends who want to do the same thing. It's scary and thrilling and ridiculous and creative. I've thought a lot about why I love to do it, especially as a recovering overachieving, grade-obsessed, worry-prone, list-making perfectionist, and the best reason I can come up with is because it's the most fun there is. And so many good things have come out of doing it that I can't even write about it without feeling the best feelings.

My friends Hailey Smith, Brett Merritt, Jake Suazo, Maclain Nelson, and I started The Thrillionaires as an improvisation troupe several years ago, and it has been one of the greatest creations and experiences of my life. We improvise theater in different styles. We get some suggestions from the audience, like the name of the play we're doing or the name of the "hit song" in the musical we're about to perform. And some individual players will get their own, different suggestions for their own characters, like a name, a personality trait, a deep fear, an unfulfilled dream, or an occupation. We get these suggestions to give us a place to start and to invite the audience in on creating the story with us. Also, it is critical for the audience to believe us when we say we haven't preplanned the plot, characters, melodies, or lyrics—not only to prove our legitimacy (because we *haven't* preplanned) but also because we want to share in the creative process with them. It's not a movie, it's a theater *experience*. We've made up plays in the genres of film noir, Oscar Wilde, Shakespeare, western, sci-fi B movie, '80s John Hughes movie, Jane Austen, and so on. We also improvise musicals (my favorite) in those same genres and other musical genres, like Rodgers and Hammerstein, operetta, rock opera, and so on, complete with original improvised songs. We don't know where the lyrics, melodies, or harmonies will go. It's the most rewarding thing to pull off because so many things could go wrong, and regularly do, and if you can win over the audience and really get them to buy into this new world you're creating on stage, you can feel how much they want you to succeed and how relieved and excited they are when you finally do.

When Maclain and Hailey first approached me about starting our own troupe, it was to experiment with this long-form theater technique and because we were all dissatisfied with waiting around to be used in other troupes, or for other acting opportunities, or to do the short-form improv games that were all more of the same and that we felt were less female-friendly. Hailey and I were both already moms at this time with husbands in graduate school, and we were very particular about what kinds of creative outlets we wanted to participate in. Typical plays rehearse and perform for several weeks, sometimes months, and we didn't have the luxury of that kind of commitment because we had already committed ourselves to lots of babies. We also wanted to collaborate. We didn't want to fight our way with other performers who only saw women as "moms" or "girlfriends" in a scene. We didn't want to just stand around and react; we wanted to explore. We had to be picky, and so we created our own opportunity to perform.

I don't think I could have anticipated how much improvisation would fill my mom bucket and how it would become the framework of how I navigated motherhood. Because the framework that facilitates effective improv parallels the framework that facilitates effective mothering, as the following principles illustrate.

1. Who you play with makes all the difference.

Players bond together and they learn good and bad habits from each other. They are judged as a team because they are creating a product together. Sounds like a family, doesn't it?

On the stage, we wouldn't be able to do what we do without each other. We've seen that, and it's painful. It's uncomfortable to everyone—the players and the audience—when someone isn't comfortable with doing improv or is just interested in getting as much stage time and self-promotion as possible. You improve in improv when you know the other players well and want them to succeed, and vice versa. Our focus when we're on stage is to set everyone up for success. We should all be looking for ways to forward the story, listen to what the other characters want, and help them get it. Egos and personal agendas to be "the lead" or "the protagonist" can't be the focus, or the show isn't as interesting.

There are all kinds of parenting theories and advice, but none of that is important if it isn't connected or doesn't relate to the individuals who call you Mom. I am a better mom when I'm concerned with setting up each individual to succeed.

2. Being overprepared is critical.

In acting, we bring everything on stage with us, everything we know about and have observed, including people, movies, books, ideas—everything. It's hard to conceal things about yourself when you're making acting choices on stage. You reveal people you know, personality traits, information you find interesting or annoying. It's very personal in that regard.

More revealing to me has been playing the "role" of mother. (I can't believe I typed that.) Because you can play like you're Mary Poppins or Shauna Valentine, but you can't keep that up forever. Sooner or later (rarely later), the kids catch on. They see you secretly binging on Lay's potato chips in the pantry, or they find the YouTube video of you singing and dancing "You Give Love a Bad Name" in a flash mob, and, maybe more quickly than you would have liked, you have revealed who you really are.

When I was teaching junior high and high school English classes, I always had a backup plan. In fact, I had an emergency substitute plan and a stack of ideas to reinforce concepts if students weren't grasping the idea, just in case. So, at least three backup plans. I had to think ahead—those students could smell fear and sense hesitancy. Then it was over, and you'd lose the class with one "*Uhhhhmmm*" that lasted too long.

Now that I've been mothering for over sixteen years, I have a backup plan for everything from food and shelter to clothing and entertainment, everything. I think that the secret to my happiness is preparing for the worst-case scenario. (Perhaps this explains my love for post-apocalyptic stories.) Truth be told, my backup plan usually ends up being "the plan" for the day. I always start the day with good intentions. "What are you doing today?" or "What's your day look like?" is a tricky question to ask. "Come what may and love it" means that your plan has to be flexible, even if you don't want it to be. But being on top of it all means adjusting, or dropping some less essential things along the way. And you usually have to make these many decisions on the fly. Improv has made me more comfortable with embracing the on-the-fly lifestyle instead of being frustrated by my beautifully planned, annotated, displayed in a new, glossy "Nate Berkus for Target" Mead binder, decorated-with-gold-stars Plan A that never sees the light of day.

When we are preparing for a show, we practice setting up locations, raising the stakes in the story, and furthering the story along. Before we step on stage, we warm up and mentally clear our minds. We are prepared in that we know what the genre is, and some characteristics or traits of the genre, but what comes out on stage is often unexpected, both to the audience and to us. Modern elements of story or narrative may creep in, blunders on names and locations may need some backtracking and justification to fit into the story, but the story moves along with the most important elements of exposition, climax, and resolution, and we try to stay as true to our original genre as we can to give an entertainingly original story.

The brass tacks of mothering require the same overall focus mingled with the same generous forgiveness in recovering from mistakes. Instead of being paralyzed by fear of a single error, the object is to recover from it as soon as possible in order to move on to the more important objective: the story.

3. Creating the right setting is important.

If our audience members are waiting in a darkened theater, having paid to see us, with a professional stage complete with great costumes and lighting and a good sound system, it prepares them for what we do and for the play they are about to see. I guarantee they have a better time than if we, say, walked into a crowded, brightly lit mall wearing regular clothes, no one having paid to see us. The shows could be identical, but the mall audience wouldn't be prepared and wouldn't be as receptive to our play. I have learned never to underestimate the power of presentation.

This is certainly true in my experience as a mother as well. I know when my "presentation" will be accepted and when it will fall on deaf ears. Topher and I recognize that taking the time to create the right setting is important when teaching kids. Just as important, I've learned that each kid responds differently at different times of the day or in different circumstances, which is interesting. It's my responsibility to play to each child's strength.

4. Know your audience.

Mothering teenagers is like doing a remote corporate show. For an actor, remote corporate shows are THE WORST because the audience is eating while you're trying to perform, so they're not really listening. They didn't pay to see you, so they're suspicious of you. (*Am I going to LIKE this? Who are these yahoos?*) You have to win them over *and* give them a show, and their focus is split because they're kind of "at work," and they kind of *have* to be there. JUST LIKE dealing with a teenager. But actors do these shows because this is where the money is. It pays off in the end, but you're sweating it THE ENTIRE TIME.

What you expect from a five-year-old is different from what you expect from a fifteen-year-old. In all the things we try to teach as mothers, from cleaning a toilet to under-standing morals and ethics, from learning to tie a shoe to learning to contribute something positive to society, ac-counting for the age, background, interests, and as many other traits as you can specifically identify will only in-crease your success.

I was once having a conversation with my husband in which I was listing all my frustrations with my boys. The criticism fell into this overall theme: They weren't listening to me. I was giving them important information (which I still stand behind as being useful, awesome instruction on how to be better prepared in life). When I had finished my tirade, Topher cautiously asked me if I would like a little advice. Desperate for a possible solution, but suspicious that he had thought about something I hadn't already con-sidered, I said yes. He told me to limit my instructions to the teenage boys to two, *maybe* three sentences delineating what I wanted them to do. He told me that he remembered what it was like to be a teenage boy, and he had been like that, too. Though I was insulted that my speeches were not being appreciated, I relented. And I really hate to admit this, but it works better his way.

5. Be confident.

In our Thrillionaire shows, each player who steps on stage adds to what has already been established. All our characters and choices spring from that original first scene and what the first two actors on stage have done. If we all had equal say, we would be negotiating and talking more than acting, which would make for a boring play. The actors starting the show need to walk on the stage with confidence and make strong, clear choices.

Parents likewise need to be confident in moving the family forward. I'm not suggesting a total dictatorship, of course; negotiation is a great life skill and has its place. But kids know when you can be persuaded. They smell weakness. They know when your defenses are down and the negotiation process is open. My kids know that when I'm stressed and weak, I can be talked into ordering pizza. They see when I'm distracted and can be persuaded to let them stay out past curfew. Being immobilized by every suggestion and whim your kids have gets you nowhere.

We can't wait to be inspired to make confident, clear choices—other professionals don't. They roll up their sleeves and get to work. There are scales to run, stretches to be made, paintings to be painted, and drills to do. Personally, I've never canceled a show because I "just wasn't feelin' it." And so it is with being a mom. There's nothing like that feeling of hearing a baby cry and not being ready to wake up, but you get yourself up and do it.

6. Be comfortable making specific choices.

When setting up a scene, I've found that it's more interesting to mime the action of carrying groceries in a bag, setting them on an imaginary table, and putting them away by establishing where the imaginary cupboards are, instead of just standing there saying, "I'm in the kitchen." Instead of saying "Oh, hello there" to someone entering the stage, it's more interesting to say, "Hello, Marjorie. I've been waiting an hour for you, so let's get started with your paperwork." Being specific is a gift, and it moves the action along. It's more interesting to watch. It's also funnier.

One of the fears about being specific is that you are locking the other person on stage into something, not being open to letting things just happen. This is a pitfall in improv, however, this waiting for someone else to do something to move the story forward. If both people are waiting, the result is a big, boring pause on stage. You have to more forward even if what comes to you is unexpected. In fact, in improv you learn to see the unexpected as the very best gift. It mixes the story up and brings out the true motives in the characters. It brings you out of your head and makes you live in the moment. The unexpected forces you to break on stage (despite the best training) and laugh, like pure joy brought to life.

Being the mom is like being the leader of managing the unexpected for the family. Being specific in a family is really important to me as a mom because it helps me get to the heart of what my kids want. Is the baby crying because he's tired, hungry, overstimulated, or hurt? Is the tween upset because she's lonely, mad, hurt, or confused? Specifics matter. Being specific also means you are doing things that are specific to your own goals as a group. When someone says, "We're the 'outdoorsy' family," what does that even mean? Do you bike? Camp? Sit outside and stare at squirrels? Being specific makes it more real. Do you celebrate holidays in a certain way or have traditions or rituals that define you or bind you together? There are many ways to be specific. Our fear of the unknown or unexpected shouldn't keep us from moving forward or making specific plans. Anticipate that something unexpected will come along because that will most definitely happen.

I am so grateful for the unexpected opportunities in my life. I'm surprised by how much of my life is ridiculous. I *imagined* a sophisticated, mysterious life, and I kind of got the opposite. It's funny, but all in all it turned out better than I could have imagined in a lot of ways—and more difficult in others, too, of course. When I was filming a parody of *The Hunger Games* trailer for the first season of *Pretty Darn Funny,* I found myself up a tree, literally, balancing on a branch, clinging to the base, trying not to slip and really hurt myself, looking down at a film crew, and I thought, *I wrote something, and now we're filming it, and then we'll have it forever. Are you kidding me?!* It felt like such a dream come true that I never would have believed I would really have the opportunity to do, and I was having so much fun. I've found myself sitting in the sleepy seaside town of Dawlish, England, running away from mean ducks and seagulls who I feared would bite my toddler boys. I've found myself in a warehouse dancing like Kevin Bacon (I wish!), simultaneously laughing at my dancing skills and frustrated that they weren't more accurate. I've found myself in the middle of Days Market, seeing a long-lost friend for the first time in years, right as my son threw up all over the floor. Life is a mix of emotions and always includes the unveiling of the unexpected.

7. Be generous with others.

We don't act in a vacuum (unless it's in a crazy sci-fi film, in which case I want to see that—and actually, now that I think about it, I want to *write* that). I have found that our performances are tied to other people. The reason why I love doing improv with the particular people I work with is because they are all generous on and off the stage. They create good opportunities and they are genuinely happy for each other's successes. The best improv plays and musicals we've had—with the best response from the audience, the most interesting stories, the best music, the most personal satisfaction—are the shows when we *all* do well, not just one or a few of us.

We all have opportunities every day to be generous—or not. We can be the one who loves more, or helps more, and certainly most mothers know the truth of that. But life is the accumulation of the memories we make with the people who were there; it's not just a list of our independent choices. In improv and in parenting, choosing to be generous when I don't have to be always creates the best art.

8. Know when to let go.

Inevitably, after the show is over and you've laughed and taken down the chairs and gathered up your stuff, you get in your car and drive home. You're coming off the high of the endorphins of being on stage, where everything happened so fast and you were so busy adjusting and performing and reacting that you didn't have time to reflect. Now it's the drive home, and all you have is time to think about what just happened.

It's so easy to be overcritical on the drive home: Why didn't I say *this* instead of *that?* If only I had made this choice, instead of that dumb one, I could have set up him to do this and her to say that and it would have been perfect! So clever and funny! Why didn't I do *that* instead! I'm the worst! It was right in front of my face and I didn't pick it up!

I've beaten myself up for things I said and didn't say, for things I did and didn't do, and for thoughts I acted on and didn't act on. But this kind of overwhelming criticism isn't useful. It hasn't made me a better actor or improviser. In fact, this line of thinking makes me less confident on stage, less helpful and available to other players, and less happy. I have to tell myself that it was a good show, that the audience had fun, that we had fun. I have to remember what we did right (we made strong choices, we made each other laugh, it was a strong story). We'll rehearse and work on improvements later, but for now we have to enjoy what we've done for more than a second.

As moms, we don't have the luxury of ever stepping off the stage. Ever. So letting go is the hardest part for me because I have to remember that sometimes I need to turn off my brain and have fun and "enjoy it," to not be in control, even when there's always something to worry about, if only a little bit, all the time. I need to pause and celebrate small victories and consciously forgive myself for mistakes.

As my kids get older, I am starting to realize that I have to let go little by little, and I don't like it. But I see that it's an important part of my job as a mom. I have to know when my kids need to make their own choices, and now and then I have to watch them fail at something and not step in to clean it up or fix it for them. This doesn't come naturally to me. I have to keep practicing.

So when moments come to "get in the car and drive home," and I worry about every little thing I've done or said wrong as a mom, I can stop and try to let go and celebrate the good. Because I've learned that we can rehearse again tomorrow.

What to Say to a Mother of Teenagers

1. Their frontal lobe hasn't fully developed yet. (This explains so much. They aren't physically able to make the best decisions—IT'S SCIENCE, not you!)

2. You're cool and smart. The reason they think you're not is you've been so busy GIVING EVERYTHING TO THEM you don't have time for anything else.

3. I'll bring food over to you right now. Which kind of chocolate do you prefer?

It's About Time

Or, If I can just make it to nap time, I think I'll be okay

My kids have habitually become ~~obsessed with~~ interested in things that I have absolutely no interest in. With my first two boys, Miles and Owen, it was Pokémon; with Phoebe, it was American Girl dolls; with Hugh, it is Legos; and with Margaret, My Little Ponies. I knew that it was important to their intellectual and emotional development to have me listen to them talk about their interests. I knew I needed to listen when they talked so they would feel comfortable talking with me about their ideas and points of view—which I knew would become increasingly important as they grew older. I wanted them to feel valued and loved and to have opportunities to talk about their own ideas in their own words. I would remind myself of all those reasons over and over again as I fought mentally to find something, *anything,* interesting about Pokémon. (*"Gotta Catch 'Em All!" Do we? Do we really gotta catch 'em all?)* So I would ask questions and listen. Something that took me one and a half kids to figure out is that it is important to know just enough to indicate that you are actually listening and absorbing the information, as uninteresting as it may be. So I memorized the Pokémon name "Charmander" and the fact that its power is fire. This fact has come in handy hundreds of times. For example, I would have this kind of conversation repeatedly:

Kid: Mom, what's your favorite Pokémon?

Me: Charmander.

Kid: Mom, who would win in a battle with asdpfoiasf and xixosnfan?

Me: I don't know, but I'd sure like to see Charmander in that battle! His fire would break that up pretty fast!

Kid: Seriously! Good one, Mom!

And so on. Substitute "Pinkie Pie" for "Charmander" and you're on your way to an informed discussion about My Little Ponies. It works (*you're welcome*). If you're going to invest in spending time with your kids, you should have some tools in your back pocket for those glazed-over moments that inevitably come. In raising kids, it's about time, after all.

My frustration with time is the unspoken but assumed hierarchy of whose time is most important in a family. I could be standing at attention in my living room, just waiting to lovingly serve my family, like a robot waiting for an order, and nothing happens. But the minute I sit down, pick up a book, or turn on the TV, they need me to do something RIGHT THAT MINUTE. Children sense weakness. They know when they can negotiate with you to let them have friends over, drive them somewhere, or go get a treat. Margaret knows that right after I pick her up from kindergarten is the best time to suggest we drive to Sodalicious "just for a little treat, Mom." If I hesitate, she knows to say, "Just real quick. It's on the way." And she's *six*. Like piranhas in the water smell blood, kids attack when they smell your presence.

My kids regularly trap me and my husband, and they're so good at it that we're consistently falling for it. They may all be cuddled together watching a movie in perfect contentment, but the second they sense one of us is walking past them, they suddenly remember they NEED A DRINK or NEED ME TO GET SOMETHING. It's as if by observing them in a nice moment, we've broken the spell. All of a sudden, our very presence alerts their brains that they're thirsty, hungry, or somehow in need of SOMETHING.

The interesting thing about time is that it is relative to each individual. As the mom, or the leader of a bunch of little individuals, I'm always working with their perceptions of time. It seems like I'm constantly telling little people to either hurry up or slow down: *Hurry up and put your shoes on. Slow down and chew your food.* At the same time, I've been very protective of my kids' time. They need time to look at the clouds, build forts, play games, make up games, imagine, and pretend. I see myself as a guardian of their time.

And I have to be conscious of my own time as well. I've often wondered why the majority of our days will not be "big-banner" days: graduations, ceremonies, or holidays. Most of our days will be random, ordinary days, many of which we will forget, but the accumulation of which will make us who we are. I've always suspected that this life was intended to be that way for a significant reason. But it wasn't until I was overwhelmed with the mundane, days-running-together feeling that I took the time to really read, think, and pray about it and find the meaning in it.

You could have a killer day at work or at home and accomplish *everything,* all the deadlines met, the laundry done, and the dishes put away. But it's never "all done"—not the housework, not the projects, not the life lessons you're teaching your kids about all the things you want them to internalize. At some point, you just have to take a deep breath and go to bed, knowing mortality is a process. Sisyphus knows what I'm talking about, pushing that rock up the hill only to have to do it again, over and over, for eternity. It's the journey that's important, and we're reminded by those ahead of us on the parenthood road to keep that in mind.

Whether we see it or not in our modern, privileged society, there is often a ritualistic way of doing work that we may view as being "beneath" us. Doing the dishes, sweeping the floor, cutting up vegetables, cleaning out a closet of unwanted or unused items—these tasks have spiritual and emotional applications. As a young mom, I was so frustrated that I didn't have time to think, or to sit and really study my scriptures or read the other books I wanted to, or to work on anything other than the demands I felt others were putting on me. (I was so excited to stay home with my first child because, with my degree in English in one hand and a baby in the other, I thought I would have time to read the literary canon at my leisure! I remember voicing that idea to my mom. She just laughed. Didn't say anything. Just laughed.) What I really wanted was to live a deliberate, meaningful life; what I felt like was a servant wasting my education and passion and days doing tasks, *not living.* But after I spent some time pondering and praying about my situation, I got my answer: *Isn't washing the dishes a time to say prayers? Isn't preparing dinner a time to think about creative projects you want to do and organize the way to do them in your mind? Isn't cleaning out a closet a time to reevaluate family time and job opportunities and visualize what to get rid of in your life, the things that don't matter? Isn't exercising the perfect time to really think about things that don't sit well with you or are bothering you and making you really mad? Isn't this a good time to solve problems? Working out and working it out?* These are ways I found time to meditate and contemplate, all while "doing."

Something that is relatively new to me is running. I never used to see exercise as a mental cleansing of sorts. I saw it as a necessary evil. Maybe because I got to a point where I literally envisioned myself running away from home, fast and free of my heavy, overwhelmed mind and tired body, I started to feel differently about it. Running and the endorphins it generated and the loud music in my ears and the oxygen coursing through my body changed the way I thought. It made me happy. I still think, as I'm putting on my running shoes, *Ugh. Can I even run one mile? Can*

I do this? And then I do it, and I'm always so glad I did. I get my best ideas when I run. I'm sure it has something to do with fresh mountain air in my lungs, the sun on my face, and the endorphins, but running clears my head. I get insight about my kids. And I have time.

I didn't always have the time and focus to run, but now I make time for it and guard that time. When I had babies and toddlers, I guarded nap time like it was holy. I would be obnoxious and put a note on the door, unplug the phone, and everything. Some exhausted mornings I would think, *If I can just make it to nap time, I think I'll be okay.*

I try to be deliberate in how I spend my time, but like everyone else, I find that the day slips away from me like sand in a sieve and it's time to start again. The accumulation of these days is the time I'm concerned with now. I remember when my pediatrician told me that a toddler's nutrition should be counted over three or four days and not in a twenty-four-hour period (no need to obsess that one day she wanted frozen peas all day and the next day only bananas). I try to think that way about a lot of my family's needs. Some days are highly focused on one child or one family need, or the housework, or a job, or a project, but the accumulation evens things out over time.

Time slips away, even while you're watching it, and with all my good intentions to teach, create moments, and make memories, I often find myself wondering, "Is it ever enough? Did I love each child for who he or she is, individually? Say everything I want to say? Are there even enough hours in the day to accomplish all of that?" I need to find a few breaks along the way to give me perspective. These come as slow revelations or discoveries, and they come in shocking moments as well. But all of these things take time.

Living in a world of clutter and chaos and shifting schedules while craving order and simplicity (and modern sleek minimalism) takes some adjustment and deep breaths. *Oh, we changed band practice to two hours earlier, didn't I tell you? Oh, I'm going to give everyone a ride and we have to fit Joelle's drums in our van. Oh, the science fair project is tomorrow and Lydia's coming over right now, didn't I tell you? We'll need some supplies.* Just constant adjusting. So I need time to decompress. Time to think so I can be deliberate and thoughtful, not just busy or filling my time doing things that I think are good, but that may not actually end up being very useful or significant in the long run. There's a dangerous temptation as a mom not to let *anything* go because it all might be important. Constantly adapting to changing needs requires keen mental focus and discipline. It also requires that we think in a calm, mentally uncluttered environment. Some people meditate, some people pray, some people look at art or walk in nature. I take what I can get.

Motherhood has changed the way I see time. I am more careful with it. I respect it more. I don't understand why time has to be so linear; I hate that aspect of it and wonder if I will ever come to terms with it. I try to extract as much joy and meaning as I can out of each stage of life. I see now that there will never be a perfect or favorite stage, but I can work to find the good and survive the bad in all stages. I love being able to talk to my sons about *Doctor Who,* to introduce them to classic movies and bands I love, to talk to them about politics in a meaningful way, and I don't have to memorize one character in these settings because I'm ~~obsessed by~~ genuinely interested in these things too. But some days I look around the house wishing I could take that chubby blond toddler to the park and push him on the swing for an hour. And on some rainy days I wish I could sit and nurse a baby and go back and forth from staring out the window to staring at the bright eyes of my perfectly content daughter. But I remember vividly days when the kids were tiny when I wished I could just run outside for an hour by myself and think and breathe deeply, and I do that now. Or days when I dreamed of putting everyone in the car and we could go to the same movie together without diaper bags and elaborate plans and negotiations about who would entertain the baby. And it turns out, I was right—that is really as great as I thought it would be. I know we all have to come to terms with time. It moves forward without our permission, which is good and bad, but that's just the way it is.

A lot of people talk about "the best years of our lives." I wonder if I believe in such a thing. During my "best years," I left my teaching career just as it was starting off, and we scrimped and saved while Topher got a bunch of degrees and training, and I grew babies and kissed foreheads and did laundry and wrote and read and laughed and did a lot of other things. I waited for things to get less overwhelming and for life to get predictable and comfortable.

And it never did.

And so I stopped waiting for that, and I changed.

Alive By 5

Or, I am, and will be forever, an amateur

I was really surprised to learn how much time I would have to dedicate to keeping my child alive. I was under the assumption that the blissful moments of reading Shel Silverstein and Hans·Christian Andersen in a comfy chair while sniffing a clean, freshly washed head would occupy most of my time. But then Owen came along, and he changed everything.

My longtime friend Eric D. Snider once wrote in his popular "Snide Remarks" column a description of Owen as a toddler:

snide remarks #282
"To Bee in Dawlish"
by Eric D. Snider
Published in the Daily Herald *on May 1, 2002*

The young lads, Miles and Owen, are 4 and 2, respectively. Miles is inquisitive and smart. Owen, meanwhile, is a force of nature. He toddles around ferociously, raging and hollering like a madman. He appears to be speaking, but the words are not from any discernible language. If he weren't so adorable, I'd assume he was evil. My best guess: He has bees in his head, and the bees are crazy.

Claire always insisted she would not be one of those mothers who put harnesses on their kids in public, but that was before she tried to navigate the tiny sidewalks of Dawlish, England, with mild-mannered Miles holding one hand and bee-headed Owen tugging at the other. And so Owen has a leash. He doesn't mind it, but he does walk at a 45-degree angle, constantly pulling against the harness as hard as he can. Dawlish is a quaint sea-side town designed by elves for use in their postcards. Everything is small and picturesque. There is a fish-and-chips shop on every corner. And the place is CRAWLING with English people, most of whom are too reserved to be entertained by Owen the unmedicated lunatic toddler.

He has bees in his head, and the bees are crazy became the phrase to describe why I became the mother I became for this particular child. The juxtaposition of these two children, twenty-one months apart, only highlighted their individuality. It was easy to recognize, early on, that I might have learned a thing or two with my first child, but I had a lot more to learn with child number 2, number 3, and so on.

The first time we took the boys to the coast of Dawlish, England, where we lived for a year while my husband was getting his master's degree, Owen ran right into the ocean. It was October and it was freezing, but he went straight in without looking back. It became apparent that he wasn't going to "learn his lesson" or get cold, frightened, or worried about any possible danger, and so Topher had to go in, retrieve him, and use his sweater to wrap up the shivering, angry toddler. He was mad at us because we had ruined his fun by saving him from the frigid water and sharp rocks.

It didn't end there. As described in Eric's article, the thought of putting a harness, a LEASH, on one of my kids had previously seemed ridiculous but quickly became my only option for keeping him safe. The streets we walked up and down every day to the play groups, to the shops, and to the park were single-file spaces. Miles was really small, just three, and Owen was eighteen months, so I needed to hold both their hands unless they were in their double stroller, which was huge and awkward. Besides which, pushing them in it didn't produce the desired effect of our outings: to get the boys worn out! Putting on the harness didn't solve all my problems, however. Owen would repeatedly try to free-fall by stiffening his entire body and leaning to get as close as he could to the ground. Or he would try to lean over the edge of the cliff by the water, or run into traffic, taking us all with him. I got used to wrapping the harness around my wrist twice and wearing sensible shoes with a solid grip so I could brace myself. I also got really good at anticipating his every move by recognizing potential danger: *There's a black swan, he's going to chase it. Here comes a pack of ducks, he's going to run toward them to the stream, but he won't see the edge and he'll run right in. He's going to try to eat that French fry off the floor. For sure he does not see that car, he just sees the kite, and he can't resist that mud puddle. It's too inviting. It's too big. He'll just lie down in it and try to swim in it.* And so on.

I learned that I couldn't be saying "NO!" to Owen all day, either. That wasn't fair. Besides, then when he *did* try to jump off a cliff and his life was on the line, if I had been saying no all day he would be deaf to it because it would be so ordinary, and he wouldn't hear me say STOP! or NO! when it really counted. (In fact, we had Owen's hearing tested four times over the course of the year because we were worried he couldn't hear us because he, well, didn't seem to be listening to us and his language was unintelligible. One doctor looked over the hearing tests and chuckled, saying, "Oh, he can hear you, all right . . .") So play groups, places where we could go and let the boys loose to paint, run, laugh, and sing with other kids became important. The park was important—anyplace to run and run and roll in the mud. We spent hundreds of hours throwing millions of stones into the sea, something Miles and Owen never got sick of doing. Now, forever, when I think of Owen as a toddler, I will see the look on his face as we crossed the last busy street into the center of town to the huge, open park, when I would let go of his hand or the leash and yell to the boys, *"Okay, RUN!"* He would always take off as fast as he could, then look back at me with sheer joy, and turn back and run and run and run.

At this stage in our parenting, Topher and I would regularly say, "Alive by 5," which reminded us that that was our number-one job.

Even if we looked like horrible parents (by putting a leash on our kid) or seemed like rude friends (by leaving a conversation midsentence to grab Owen from jumping onto train tracks), or seemed paranoid (we'd lock all doors and windows at all times while inside the house), it didn't matter to us. We weren't messing around. This was a kid who dove into the ice-water bucket at the ward party, climbed on top of the refrigerator at age eighteen months and ate the centers out of two packs of Oreos, and stole the minister's flute and ran off with it during the Christmas program at the Methodist play group. Our job was to put out fires, constantly.

Owen was the kid who, the first week in our new home, bent the outside metal decorative swirls on our backyard awning with his bare hands so he could use them to climb to the roof to walk

Side Rant

Isn't there supposed to be an internal indicator that makes you want to preserve and protect your life? You know, similar to the physical internal clock that keeps your heart beating and keeps your lungs working even if you don't think about it? Something that mitigates risky behavior? I was disturbed by this lack of impulse control when my kids were toddlers, but now that they are teenagers, I'm even more surprised by it because they have experienced cause and effect before. I feel like, by now, their brains should be fully developed—but they're not. My teenage boys are taller than me, but they WANT to do risky things.

around and, you know, take a look. When four-year-old Miles matter-of-factly told me, "Owen's on the roof, Mom," I didn't believe him. We had bought the house mainly because it had a fenced-in backyard, a luxury I had dreamed about to give me a little peace of mind. (That peace of mind was a fantasy, an illusion that didn't last.) We hadn't been there more than a few days. There was surely enough in the backyard to keep him busy, but he did regularly climb things. In our previous home I did have to remove the kitchen drawer knobs because he used them to climb the shelves and refrigerator to raid my not-so-secret treat cupboard. So when Miles warned me, I immediately ran outside with baby Phoebe on my hip, dashing around the house trying to find Owen. I yelled and yelled his name, and he finally came walking over the crest of the roof really casually, like, "What?" I screamed for him to stop right where he was, sit down, and scoot on his bum toward the edge. I didn't have the heart to go meet my neighbors for the first time by asking them if I could borrow their ladder because my two-year-old had climbed onto the roof. I had my pride. So I had a screaming baby, a stool, me on my tippy toes, a confused toddler on the roof with an expression like, *What is she so upset about? I'm fine. I mean, I'll do what she says, but why is she so upset?* And some random neighborhood kids and a calm Miles all watching me. Judging me.

After that, I reveled in the humiliation of knowing that I would feel like an amateur mother forever. I focused on keeping the kids alive and all of us as happy as possible.

This took a lot of negotiating and reevaluating at every step. I like to think that those early years were good for me as a mom because they made me lighten up really quickly and not take myself too seriously when I could have, very easily.

It was never a boring day. Sometimes monotonous, but certainly not boring. It's not like I knew what was coming next.

Owen is now fourteen, and he loves to play football, he's smart, and he is still the sweetest boy you'll ever meet. He will regularly wrap his arms around me and say, "How was your day, Mom? Anything I can do for you?" He's a charmer. He has an inner calmness, but he still has that fun streak in him that organizes games for the neighborhood, shows me funny YouTube videos (some of which are him doing flips off sand dunes at Scout camps), and laughs at my reaction as I watch.

But as calm and sweet as he is now, I still tense up whenever he calls, *"Hey, Mom! WATCH THIS!"*

Bring It On, Noon!

The following is an excerpt from my journal from 2009. I was still adjusting to keeping five children alive. I was feeling the whole "The days are long but the years are short" feeling.

It's 10 am and I have already gotten 2 kids fed, dressed, blow-dried Phoebe's hair (four days of frizzy braid hair and I couldn't take it any longer), looked for Phoebe's coat, gave Phoebe the "money doesn't grow on trees" speech when she finally admitted she thinks she lost it somewhere, some time ago, scriptures read, and prayed off to school, helped Miles throw up, made him a bed on the couch, fed Margaret 3 breakfasts (one was a Creamie), made four beds, cleaned marker off three comforters, two sheets, and three pillowcases, drove Hugh to preschool, answered a frantic call from Owen to go to the school because the Read-a-thon sheets were due today (a fact I told him last night and again this morning, but he had argued against passionately), drove to the school to find two Read-a-thon sheets in two boys' messy desks, filled them in, signed them, turned them in, reluctantly put off a PTA member who wants me to mime a turtle's dialogue in the Dr. Seuss Read-a-thon assembly on Tuesday by saying "email me . . . ," came home, checked my emails, balanced my checkbook, laughed really hard at Kacy's blog, read angry comments on my sister-in-law's blog, and formed three different responses to aforementioned comments in my head as I folded and put away laundry, made Miles and Margaret a smoothie, emptied the dishwasher, loaded the dishwasher, wiped down the kitchen with a semi-clean rag, put on "Yo Gabba Gabba" for Margaret and wrapped her up in 2 blankets (because the smoothie made her "cooldeez!") and put away magazines, mail, and schoolwork in files.

Bring it on, Noon.

You've Got Some Advice, Settle Down

Or, Dancing in the rain like no one's watching while
following my heart and living outside the box while
seizing the day and keeping calm and carrying on
and not sweating the small stuff

Women are constantly given an abundance of conflicting advice, the combination of which is not super helpful. I can get really worked up about advice, too. I'm a firm believer that there's a lot of good out there to be found and that we should all be looking for it. There are a lot of self-help books by smart people who have identified really great ways to become a better person, and I'm all for that. I personally love to read books about creativity and the creative process, like *The Artist's Way,* and philosophy books from authors like Kierkegaard and C. S. Lewis. I think Oprah does a lot of good and searches for good. She gave all those teachers cars, for crying out loud! She told me, years ago, to drink more water, and I just barely started listening a few months ago and wish I had listened earlier. I can get a little intense about goal setting and overwhelm myself by setting unrealistic expectations, like the year I signed up for the elementary, middle school, AND high school PTAs. That's a lot of meetings. Classic rookie mistake. No one should ever have to go to that many meetings, as I had to learn the hard way.

As I clunkily transition from one stage of life to the next, I want to know what others' experiences are and how they might help me avoid pain and suffering (and meetings) and, most of all, regret. I want to look back at my life with as few regrets as possible. (As I get older, I just want to look back at my life with peace, regrets or not.) But there's one aspect that Oprah (and I acknowledge that she's an easy target; she's the most rich, famous, and infamous as they come) and others with "the answers" to everything fail to acknowledge. While they're telling us how to have a better life, a richer life, a simpler life, a more fulfilled life, an organized life, whatever, they don't seem to see that it would be impossible to follow all of their good ideas simultaneously, as superior as those ideas may be.

It is simply not possible to follow ALL the good advice available out there. And trying to pursue all the great ideas would take a hefty toll. It gets a little ridiculous, when you stop and think about it. For example, I remember watching when Oprah was doing a "favorite things" show. (And, for the record, I'm never going to buy a candle that costs more than $100. Ever. Even if I have one million dollars. Even a candle for $25 keeps me walking right past it. It's wax! It's not like there's gold in it. And if there is, don't burn gold. That's wasteful.) Anyway, Oprah made a comment about these bedsheets she loved—I think they had a thread count I didn't realize existed and they were made from puppy tears and childhood memories—but they were really soft, and she made the comment that she loves the feeling of fresh sheets, so she has her sheets changed every three days. At that point even the guest on the show gave her a disapproving look and said something like, "Yeah, shooooot, most people aren't going to do that." I think that's such a funny, specific memory of Oprah because she was genuinely surprised that most people wouldn't change their sheets every three days. She clearly doesn't change the bedding herself in any of her numerous homes. She kind of laughed at herself at the same time she realized that maybe she was having an "Oprah moment."

I use this example to remind myself that there are all kinds of tasks, ridiculous as well as helpful, that we could be giving ourselves to do, from changing our sheets every three days to drinking more water, from meditating to "saying yes" in life, from "leaning in" to empowering ourselves, from facing our fears to taking ourselves on "artist dates." None of them are wrong or bad, but the combination is ridiculous.

So how do we know which advice to take? As Latter-day Saint women, we know who we follow, but there are so many ways to live a righteous life. How do we know we are on the right path for US? And as we transition from parenting phase to parenting phase, to fit the needs of our families and ourselves, how do we best adjust, when constant adjustment is the rule, not the exception?

Where finding advice is concerned, I have to remember

to be careful with the Internet. I know I sound like such a mom in saying that, but it needs to be stated in a book about being a mom. And yes, it makes me feel socially irrelevant and old-fashioned, the same way I feel when I write out a check, but I feel the truth of it in my perimenopausal, cracking bones. I'm among the first batch of mothers to use the Internet while mothering. It's a "first pancake" kind of thing where we just have to get through it in order to make sense of it. Navigating all the information and technology will be easier for our kids, thanks to us, right? (I'd like to think that we'll be interviewed in years to come on shows like *Katie* and *Good Morning America* on what it was like for us firsties, just trying to figure it all out. I imagine it will be a lot like "the greatest generation" talking to Tom Brokaw about World War II, only instead of "the greatest generation," we'll be referred to as "the technologically inept generation," and it's not WWII, it's the Information Age.) Yes, the bombardment of social media is a new, unprecedented way to live and we are the first generation to deal with it. This is a topic fit for its own international summit, but suffice it to say, we are the leaders of this. We're the first to deal with it, we can set the tone and determine what the conversations are, so what legacy will we leave? How will we lead?

Women need to make connections and to know that we're not invisible and that we're not going it alone. That's what we crave, and I think that's why we're constantly looking for and giving each other advice.

It's hard to navigate through all the information and

find useful, helpful advice or healthy perspectives because so much of it is about choosing up sides and berating women for being on one side or the other of some arbitrary line.

Mothering while sifting through massive amounts of information about everything from parenting to self-esteem to empowerment to social change is daunting. Somehow we've set ourselves up in our culture to all be experts. Because we've read a lot on the Internet and we're super good at Googling stuff and reading the first and last paragraphs of important articles linked on Twitter, we present ourselves as authorities instead of exchanging ideas. While there are some people whose opinions I value, these are people whom I seek out in person. In real life. (Or, as the kids say, IRL. Or they used to. Just kidding, I don't know what the kids say.)

We've created a culture of people who really think you're dying to know which Muppet the online Buzzfeed survey says they are, or how they really feel about religion and politics and parenthood (the irony of that last part is not lost on me). *Dying* to know. This is the situation and the climate in which we live. Do we really think we're going to change anyone's mind? Do we really think that people come to the Facebook table ready and anxious to read viewpoints contrary to their own? Or do we read "the other side" of the issue and get mad and think of how we will respond and cleverly put down that idea or, worse, the individual personally? Are we trying to show how enlightened we are? Or right? Or educated? Or whatever? How is this an exchange of ideas?

What if we all cut each other some slack in this area and got more of the information we crave: How do you live a Christlike life amid morally ambiguous, judgment-call situations? How have you been successful? Do you have any regrets? How do you decide? Why do you feel passionately about this? What is your experience? These are more interesting questions, anyway.

Finding solutions to our problems and questions is a deeply personal pursuit. We shouldn't just passively accept what someone else is willing to say, even if it's from a really good source. Brother Hugh Nibley made an interesting connection between accepting what

Side Rant

Can't you just tell which links people are dying for you to click on to "defend" or to "fight against" sweeping generalizations the authors have made? I hate feeling like a pawn in all of that. Pundits, commentators, bloggers, and celebrities are polarizing and take strong positions for what purpose? To sell books. To get page views. To make money. To gain power and influence and status. As a result, they are fueling the "mommy wars" and continually pitting women against women. They create a divisive environment, which for most of us generates a sense of helplessness to do anything about the horrific situations we are in politically, educationally, or religiously.

our Church leaders say and our personal responsibility to discover for ourselves:

"This authority business is a dodge. The idea is that every man must answer for himself, must decide for himself. Every president of the Church has repeatedly emphasized that. But it's so much easier to let someone else make up our minds. Let the prophets do our righteous deeds for us; if they tell us what's what, that lets us off the hook. Brigham Young has a wonderful quotation on this: 'There are some Latter-day Saints who say "If it is all right with the brethren, it is all right with me."' But that, he says, is not enough. We must decide what is virtuous and what is not because we can't ride into the kingdom on someone else's coattails."

Nibley also emphasized that we have a lot of sources for the best advice for

Side Rant

Some people never get worked up about things and stay apathetic, and some always get worked up. I have a lot of passionate opinions about a lot of things, but not every idea deserves the same emphasis. How do you know what to focus on? I can't invest time and energy caring about everything on a level 10. I can't parent as if every issue from picking up the Legos off the floor, to getting good grades, to going to church, to cleaning the bathroom deserves a level-10 emphasis. We all have to pick our battles. But does it always need to be a public battle?

our personal situations, but it requires some work to find that advice.

"The fact is that Latter-day Saints 'will not search knowledge, nor understand great knowledge, when it is given unto them in plainness, even as plain as word can be' (2 Nephi 32:7). They simply are just not interested. How little we know about things. How little we want to know. The information is there, far more abundant than we have been willing to realize, if we will only reach out for it. To wait for a revelation on the subject is foolish until we have exhausted all the resources already placed at our disposal."

I think the best advice is simple. I like what President Dieter F. Uchtdorf says: "There is a beauty and clarity that comes from simplicity that we sometimes do not appreciate in our thirst for intricate solutions." Some of the best advice I've ever received came from my husband, who tells me (repeatedly) to "sleep on it" before I respond to a particularly sensitive or hot Facebook post, email, or blog. This is good advice that not everyone takes.

On my wedding day, hoping to create a magical and tender moment with my father, I asked him if he had any advice for me, his oldest daughter and first child to get married. He didn't. When I pressed him on the issue (I really wanted my dramatic father-daughter wedding-day moment), he simply said, "Be nice. You know how you can get." And, as exhibited by my writing it right here, I have not forgotten that timeless advice, almost twenty years later. Yes. "Be nice." I know how I can get.

Shocking Moments in Motherhood

Or, Now I expect the unexpected because
I've been surprised too many times

Before I became a mom, I knew that some areas of motherhood would be difficult for me. I thought a lot about how I was going to clean up vomit without throwing up myself, and how I was going to pretend that Elmo's voice wasn't completely grating, and how I would have to negotiate power struggles. But you can only anticipate so much. I've had a few truly shocking moments in my time as a mother that I didn't see coming. You know, those realizations like a slap in the face that come on a seemingly regular Tuesday without warning, leaving you changed for better or worse. Here are just a few.

Grow a Full Human Body inside Your Body and Then Get That Body out of Yours? This Is Reasonable?

One of those moments came when I was pregnant with my firstborn, Miles. I remember waking up from a Sunday nap (it's easy for me to remember this moment because it was when "Sunday" meant "nap day," so it's obvious I didn't have kids yet), and I looked at my growing abdomen and tried to imagine what the baby looked like, how big it was. And then it hit me: *This baby is only going to get bigger, and bigger, and THEN it's going to come out. It has to. And it will be BIG. Inside of me, then out.* It wasn't like I didn't know how babies developed or how they were born, it was that it struck me that this was happening, now. The decision had been made, the die had been cast, this was it. It was going to be painful. Soon. And there was nothing to do about it. It seemed weird. That was the first hint I had that my body was largely out of my control now.

What You Shouldn't Expect When You're Expecting Because Expectations Are Exhausting.

In this book, I have consciously decided not to write about all of the shocking things that happen when you actually give birth and in the following weeks. It's too much. It's like when I learn about menopause, and I think maybe it's better that I just not know because it's a lot, and no one is ever ready for it. Being a woman is full of surprises!

So, back to the point: I had another shocking realization soon after this first one. I had given birth to Miles (and while I was pushing I distinctly remember thinking, *Women KNOW how this feels and they still CHOOSE to have another one?!*) and Owen came along twenty-one months later. I tried to take what I had learned about Miles and apply it to Owen, only to realize that each kid is like starting anew, a complete "do-over." It seemed as I went further on in mothering, especially as other kids subsequently came along, juuuuuuust as I thought I might have something figured out (just explain it logically, be firm, and he will eat what you give him), another kid would—get this—have a completely different personality and blow up my theory. What worked for one kid didn't for the next, and so on. After that, nothing shocked me. I expected the unexpected.

This was an exhausting thought, though, especially in practice. For example:

Miles was so scared to learn to ride a bike. He was a smart kid who had things figured out early on. He could name all the planets in our solar system, in order, at age two (*fun at parties!*) and his obsession with all things space and science was entertaining and made him a very methodical, logical child. When people would ask if he'd like to be an astronaut when he grew up, he would emphatically reply, "We'll send Owen up into space and I'll be the guy who stays on the ground and controls the space station." (These were their roles and he had identified them early on.) So when it came time for Miles to learn to ride a bike, he already knew about speed and how an object in motion tends to stay in motion and all of that. He wanted to be in control, but he knew things could and would go wrong. So it was naturally a hard thing for him to let go and ride the bike. There was a lot of practice and tears, because this was the kid who KNEW we were going to have to let go of the bike as we ran alongside in order for him to ride on his own. We didn't lie to him, and he couldn't forget the mechanics about how this whole learning-to-ride-a-bike thing was going to need to go, and the anticipation was heavy for the poor little guy. He eventually did it. He learned, but he never really loved it— but hey, parenting checklist down. (I think all parents have the responsibility to teach their kids to ride a bike, tie their shoes, and swim, and to get their teeth fixed. I don't know where I picked these things up, but there you go.)

So when it was Owen's turn to learn to ride a bike, I was dreading it. Topher had gone out of town, and I was at my mom and dad's home and I thought I should just get it over with. My dad is a little excited about bike riding, to say the least. It was our family pastime growing up to work in the yard on Saturdays, then hop on our bikes and go for a long family bike ride. (I think Dad liked it that people would point and yell, "Are all those kids YOURS?" as a train of seven of us passed by on the neighborhood streets of Lincoln, Nebraska.) So, as a grandpa, he had collected from thrift stores a bunch of bikes, enough so that each grandkid could ride one when they came over. He offered to teach Owen, and I was very relieved. We identified the right-sized bike for Owen, told him to get on the bike, and then he got on and . . . took off. He started peddling, went up the street, and kept going. We cheered him on and laughed because we kept waiting for him to fall over, look back, or slow down, but he never did. He kept going. First try, that was it—he had it.

The Holy Grail of Motherhood Is Mediocrity.

What came next was my reluctant acceptance of the shocking degree of mediocrity that I became accustomed to, and even strove for, in order to survive caring for small children. There is not enough time, but more importantly not enough mental focus, possible for me to make my home like Martha Stewart would have it. Those craft projects alone are rigorously intense and often have more than twenty steps apiece. They take focus and uninterrupted time. The recipes are the same. "Quick and Easy" and "Crockpot Meals" are the most pinned on Pinterest for a reason. *Good enough* becomes a worthy goal.

It's not like I didn't start out wanting to excel at motherhood. In fact, I remember fearing mediocrity. FEARING it. Yeah, can you imagine? But you *learn* some things about yourself when you're rushing to the elementary school to pick up your kindergartener forty-five minutes late because you forgot it was an early-out day. You *sense* some things about yourself as you hide behind a piano, where your son will not see you, in order to listen to his rock band practice (*what have I become?*), sitting there, not being seen, so he won't be embarrassed by YOU, and so you can most effectively fight the strong physical urge to sing. You *really* face some exciting things about yourself when you realize that your thirteen-year-old son has been hiding in the pantry patiently for twenty minutes, just waiting for you to open the door so he can scare you. And then he does. And the look of delight on his face as you scream out of sheer terror, yes, that will show you some things about yourself. I thought I could have it all together and keep it all together at the same time, but I guess there must be balance in the universe, so because motherhood is so meaningful and good, it also has to be messy and embarrassing. I guess this is my way of "balancing it all."

Who Knew That a Fourteen-Year-Old, Non-Blood Relative Held the Key to My Mental Wellness in the Palm of Her Hand?

I didn't realize that babysitters would hold such power over me, casually holding the state of my mental well-being in the palms of their sweaty, adolescent hands. There's a scripture that says the value of a virtuous woman is far above rubies; and in my mind, the value of a good babysitter is far above any perfectly cut diamond. The paid hands that rock the cradle rule the world.

I have found a couple of great babysitters over the years, and they could ask me for a kidney tomorrow and I would gladly give them one. I didn't anticipate that nego-tiating time, payment, expectations, and schedules would be such a nebulous process. No one prepared me for the uncertain "Whatever you think . . ." when I asked how much she charges per hour, knowing there is a correct an-swer that she's too uncomfortable at age thirteen, fifteen, or seventeen to give, but that holds the key to her accepting babysitting gigs in the future. Do I guess? Should I shoot high? Low? I'm locking in a contract here for her future availability, and the difference of a few dollars might be the difference between "Oh, she's not here right now" and "I'll be right over!" My excitement over going out to do something fun (or even just to drive around in a car by myself eating chili cheese fries) was always tempered by the challenge of finding a babysitter. It's quite a defeating, soul-crushing blow to get to number 7 on the babysitting list to be shot down, for whatever reason. I questioned my state as a mother: *Are my kids this bad? Is everyone really busy? I thought I paid well. I have treats! I always have good treats!* It creates a more frantic state than the one you were in that caused you to need a babysitter in the first place!

On the same note, when my kids grew up and could be trusted to babysit, this was a game changer that was better than I imagined. With my own kids I could insist on a clean kitchen, a picked-up living room, and enforced bedtime without fearing they wouldn't come back again. They *have* to—they live here. Ha! Sweet victory!

I Love You So Much That if Someone Tried to Hurt You I Could Kill Them with My Bare Hands, and I'm Not a Violent Person.

That Mother Bear instinct is no joke. About four months after my first baby was born, I heard about a child abduction, and it was then I realized that I would do anything to protect this soft, pink, helpless child of mine as I imagined what I would actually do if someone tried to take my baby. And I still would do what I imagined then.

Everyone Assumes I'm Lying or Withholding Some Deep-Seated Resentment When I Tell Them I'm Really Happy and Not Secretly Wishing I Was Someone Else.

I think every mom has a moment or two in her life that shocks her in a way that she's able to see outside of herself for a minute. In that minute, she realizes in a very personal, intimate way what being a mom means for her.

In my early years of mothering, I tried to meet basic needs, at the encouragement of my mother. She was good to tell me not to forget to stick to the basics and give up worrying about anything else. That was really helpful because I am the girl who wants to be involved in every project and go to every party. I was horribly social and fed on lists made, tasks done, and praise. So I had to adjust. I remember a time that I recognized where that adjustment had taken me.

All my kids had the flu and I had just discovered *Friday Night Lights* online, which was really exciting for me. (This may reveal my adjusted level of what constituted excitement.) I would watch some TV, dole some medicine out, watch some more, get someone a drink, watch some more, then kiss a forehead back to sleep. My husband, who was working two jobs and going to school full-time, was gone (he was always gone), and I was pregnant (I was always pregnant), and my rock star brother, James, called to talk. He was in Paris on tour with his band, Maroon5, and he wanted to tell me about Lenny Kravitz's mansion and how cool it was, and we talked about music and his travel. And he was so kind, not bragging, just checking in on me. We had a great visit. It meant so much to me. And I was so big, and I looked like such a mess, and the house smelled harsh like Clorox, and I sat and really took inventory. With Tim Riggins paused on my computer screen, I thought, *All right, Lisa. This is where your life's decisions have led you. This is it. He's never going to be home more. It's always going to be all-consuming—you're always going to go to bed really tired. You're probably never going to be a VIP guest at Lenny Kravitz's mansion in Paris. And a lot of other things.* I sat there thinking, taking inventory of where I was, who I was, and who I was with, for a long time. And I was happy.

How to Appear Smart to Your Children
(Answer: anticipate the questions you can actually answer)

All kids ask a lot of questions. It's a thing. If you're prepared to answer the following questions with some basic level of authority (in a pinch, just Google some facts about them to have a working knowledge), you'll appear somewhat intelligent to your children. (Anything that helps sustain our authority, right?) There are too many possible questions to list them all, but the following is a good working list that I would bet my 1970s rambler home they'll ask.

1. Why is the sky blue?
2. How is a rainbow made?
3. Where do tornadoes come from? (I realize now that a lot of these are weather related, so studying meteorology is a big bonus with kids.)
4. How many people live on Earth?
5. How does a tree grow from a little seed?

They'll also ask a lot of questions that are subjective, like, "Who would win in a battle: Superman or Spiderman?" or, "Would you rather fly or be invisible?" And a lot of deep, meaningful questions, like, "Why are there so many wars?" Those are tough questions, and you're on your own answering them, so it's nice to know that some questions can actually be answered. Basically, show off with the right answers when you can.

Bonus Tip: Don't panic when you ask your kids simple questions that they claim they don't know the answer to. "Why didn't you hand in this assignment if you did it?" "Why didn't you put away your laundry when you said you did?" "Why do you smell like taco meat?" "Why did you do that?" All kids claim not to be able to answer such questions. Questions are hard.

Is Everyone Just Humoring Me?

Or, Just humor the mom in the spray-painted shoes

The second season of *Pretty Darn Funny* was nominated for several web awards, and the other producers and I were really excited and encouraged by this, so we knew we had to go to the awards presentations to celebrate and to make connections. (I'm still unsure how this works. All the attendees, especially actors, just want to talk about their own projects, so who is there looking to work with someone else? Isn't everyone just looking for funding for his or her own stuff? I'm going to have to think about that some more.) I had never been to an awards show before. I already had a dress that would work, but I needed to jazz it up for Vegas and the red carpet. (I say "jazz it up" unironically. Clearly I need help.) I consulted with my sister Amanda, an excellent, super-cool stylist for pretty and fancy people, and she told me that since the dress was simple, I should go overboard on the gold, which she reassured me would work. (I find it expedient in matters of fashion and hair to defer completely to experts.) I didn't have gold shoes, and I didn't have time to go shopping, but I thought I could just spray-paint some heels I owned that I never really wore. I spray-painted them and tried them out for three hours at church, where they held up perfectly. I felt pretty good about myself. *Suckers who buy gold shoes when they could spray-paint them,* I thought, congratulating myself for my frugality and my foresight for testing them out.

Fast-forward to Vegas days later, and our *Pretty Darn Funny* group of creators and spouses found ourselves wandering around the winding Rio hotel and casino, trying to find the right banquet hall. Not wanting to be late for our red carpet "time slot" (So exciting! Who knew there was such a thing!), we rushed and ran. I composed myself while waiting for our turn on the red carpet and looked down at my shoes. Big chunks of gold had flaked off, and the result was a ridiculous patch of pink and gold, but mostly the ugly pink I had tried to cover up. I'm not saying that it was super embarrassing because (*sigh*) I've been through worse, or that it was even that funny. It just seemed inevitable that something like that would happen. I knew that I couldn't just dress up for an awards show like a regular person who belonged there. *Oh, hey, everyone! Just humor the mom in the spray-painted shoes.*

There is humor in the idea that people are humoring me. I'm sure there is, but it is still infuriating. I am a loud extrovert who physically struggles to NOT talk to strangers in grocery lines and elevators—at the insistence of my introverted friends, who plead, "Really, it's so uncomfortable. I would hate that. It's the worst! Don't do it. Resist the urge." I am sometimes good and sometimes not so good at using my inside voice and feigning neutrality on possible hot topics so as to make others around me more comfortable. But I cannot overstress how difficult this level of restraint really is for me. Because even when I think I'm doing a good job, I find out later that others (with good manners) are humoring me, which makes me think I should have just used my regular voice and facial expressions after all.

I have this inner dialogue all the time when I'm talking with my kids. Do I "tone it down," or just act like myself? When I do something like singing or doing "interpretations" of songs (as in, acting them out while dancing), I have flashbacks of sleepovers with my friends being interrupted by my dad, who would flip on the light switch at the top of the stairs and walk down to the basement, forgetting there were friends in sleeping bags all over the floor, in his caftan (you read that right: a long nightshirt, a very European and Middle Eastern thing, and one of the many things my father adopted throughout his decades of international travel, others including taking off shoes before entering the house, thanks to the Japanese, and giving up still water for Pellegrino, thanks to the French), with his hair sticking up, wiping the walls (he was always wiping down the walls) with a wet rag, apologizing when he realized his intrusion, explaining that he was down here at four in the morning because he had to "call Japan."

My dad would also offer me and my siblings $1 to go up to strangers in Pizza Hut and ask them for a slice. When we learned the value of a dollar and, simultaneously, learned the diminishing value of our dignity and started taking him up on the offer, he stopped daring us so much.

In public settings, I try not to embarrass my kids too

much, but then an opportunity will present itself and it just *seems right* to do or say something. When I asked Owen (age fourteen) to tell me *when* I've embarrassed him, he said quickly, "Every day." Seems oddly vague to me. When I pressed the issue and asked him the most embarrassing thing I've done, he said, "That time last Halloween . . . when you said hi to my friends." I asked for details, hoping for a more specific example, one that I would actually remember, but this is what I do—who I am. My very salutations to his peers *(shudder)* are enough. There it is. I admit that I know I embarrass him when I tell him I washed his football "costume" and not uniform, or call it "rehearsal" instead of practice, or "intermission" instead of halftime, but these are honest mistakes, and I don't mean to make them; I don't lose any sleep over them, either. I kind of think it's my job to embarrass my children, if just to give them good stories to tell their friends and kids of their own one day, as a contest of "who had it worse," or "which parent was the most embarrassing." I can dream.

I know I have to save my energy and focus for the discussions that matter most. I can't insist on everything, and I can't go off on a lecture about everything. I've got to pick my battles. Everyone knows that. But I've got to pick my battles AND my character, motivation, tone of voice, and emphasis. It's a lot. The emotional temperatures of all your kids bubble up around you as a mom and you're either responding to those feelings and reactions or absorbing them. That's not nothing.

Becoming a mother is an exercise in becoming invisible in a lot of ways and learning to work backstage. Being cool or relevant is overrated anyway, right? And it's totally subjective. For someone like me, who was always a little too eager to please and too hyper, with a touch of "too nerdy to be cool," I like to think it's subjective. *Relevant, shmelevant!* I know I've crossed the line into true irrelevance because I can feel it when my kids call my favorite band, The Police, "oldies," or when I see a picture of Sting and I reluctantly admit that, yes, he's looking kind of old, but I don't care. Sting is to me what Johnny Mathis is to my mother. And now I understand the circle of life.

When I was explaining my existential crisis at age twelve (yeah, explains a lot) in great detail to my fifteen-year-old son, who had innocently asked a question about existentialism, he (you'll never guess) spaced off! When I caught him, I realized that he was trying his best to humor me about my existential crisis. It all seemed ridiculous. I see the same look when I say "My Zumba ladies," or my "PTA art ladies" or other categories of friends. It seems like something a mom would say. Like the way my mom says "gals." I say "ladies."

Sometimes it's not anything we do, it's just our very being or presence that embarrasses our children. What are we supposed to do with that? *(Exploit it, that's what. That's the answer to my not-so-rhetorical question.)* Teach them to laugh at themselves, or at least at you.

I've come to learn through many uncomfortable

conversations throughout the years that it's not just my kids who are humoring me. (Forty years of lively, outgoing, extroverted conversation starters are bound to bring as many misses as hits.) A lot of people avoid humor or are uncomfortable with its many forms because they equate it with being mean or teasing or being daft or light-minded. But I have a hard time relating to people who can't take a joke or who take themselves too seriously because I think it's a form of pride. There is a difference between making fun of someone and making fun of things we *do* that are wrong, ridiculous, or unusual. I realize that it's a fine line many times, but that line is really funny and really worth it in the end.

There's a great case to be made for humor in our lives. It's disarming, it's a good way to manage stress, it's universal, it's a highly creative skill that connects both hemispheres of the brain, it's a way to engage others that's nonthreatening, and it helps people listen to what you're really saying. Also, "playing the fool" is a great Shakespearean literary tool and way to hide behind humor in order to speak the deepest and hardest truths. Shakespeare, in *As You Like It,* said, "The fool doth think he is wise, but the wise man knows himself to be a fool." (Also, who is the fool in Shakespeare's *King Lear?* It's not the jester.) I'm not saying all humor does all of this every time, or that most humor goes deep to the heart, but it is a good coping mechanism and a healthy way to express frustrating, hard, difficult, impossible things and a way to cast a light on issues and things we think are important but aren't.

Pretty Darn Funny is full of revealing the ridiculous aspects of motherhood and making fun of how seriously we take PTA fund-raising, how we compete over who's the busiest, how living a Pinterest-worthy life is a lot of work and sometimes, after all our best efforts, not even possible. And, ultimately, it's about how motherhood isn't just an idealized dream filled with blissful moments but a lot of hard work and humbling circumstances. When I was the only one pregnant (and beautifully bloated) with a third child at my ten-year high school reunion, talking with really accomplished friends I hadn't seen in years, and my buddies Wendy and Cimony nonchalantly pointed to my two little boys, who were spraying people with the water fountain, I just smiled and said, "Where are those boys' parents? They really should keep a better eye on their kids. Huh. Where could they be?" Then I wandered off with Wendy and Cim, who played along because they're always up for a good laugh. Because, really, what's the alternative? I'm with Marjorie Hinckley: I'd rather laugh because crying gives me a headache.

When my kids were babies, I was really mindful about how much I talked with them and what tone of voice I used, what I said, if I made eye contact, all of the baby development things that encourage language acquisition, foster vocabulary, and create a sense of emotional well-being. As they got older, it became easier to forget those things, including making them laugh, or at least laughing *with* them every day. Making a baby laugh is super easy. Babies aren't that clever. But the audience gets tougher to crack as they get older, especially if you're not going to sink to their level with the potty humor route (again, it's too easy). This is not a prescriptive book, and I'm not going to try to give tips on how to make your kids laugh because I'm not even that good at it. But I will offer a warning: There is a fine, fine line between being funny and trying too hard. I've stepped over that line enough times to know how uncomfortable it is to live here, but I see that it's home now. I fail a lot more than I succeed. I've used my best material on my unappreciative kids—voices, accents, characters, dances—and it's still more misses than hits.

I'm self-aware enough to know that I'm being ridiculous and crossing some trying-too-hard lines when I try to sing them a song in the style of Mary Poppins (or "Sherrie Bobbins") to get them to pick up their rooms, or when I pretend like I'm the new tutor brought in to organize the schoolwork to get them to see what organization looks like, or when I act like a robot when they keep asking me the same question over and over to teach a lesson about not breaking Mom by overloading her with requests for information. I know I'm trying too hard. They think I don't, but I know exactly what I'm doing ~~most~~ some of the time because I'm humoring them, too.

Not Really Shocking, but Still Surprising Moments in Motherhood

Or, More things I didn't see coming that I now accept with a quiet, deflated resolve

Not all moments in mothering are truly shocking. A lot of people, often compassionate mothers pushing carts in the aisles of grocery stores, try to warn us of what's ahead before these little bundles of joy are placed in our arms and we enter a new phase in our life. And maybe they forgot to tell us the surprising-but-not-shocking because nothing fazes them anymore. I don't know. Sometimes I set my clocks back to convince my kids to go to bed earlier, I count cereal as a balanced meal because it's "fortified with vitamins and minerals," and I consider running through the sprinklers equivalent to taking a bath. My what's-normal-in-mothering meter may be off. The following moments weren't necessarily "shocking," but they were surprising nonetheless.

Target Is a Great Oasis for Escape, but It's Also a Pretty, Pretty Trap.

I was surprised, and I suspect a lot of women were, by how large a part Target would play in our lives. Not only is it a place where you can buy both milk and a pair of shoes, both laundry detergent and a modern side table, but it is also a respectable place of escape. It is justifiable to get out of the house with the excuse that you're just going to "grab some diapers and wipes," when what your soul really craves is a place where you can wander and look at some beautiful things and maybe come home with an impractical necklace or new ideas for how to completely remodel your bathroom with new towels, rugs, and other accessories that moments before you didn't know you needed and now you *crave with every fiber of your being.* I realized that I was falling into the Target cult when I knew when the different departments had their markdowns, and I got excited when guest designers like Liberty of London rolled out a line of clothing or bedding. A little too excited. Not wanting to be so invested, I tried to break up with Target by mixing it up at Shopko, but their empty rows and lonely, random markdowns depressed me. I love you and I hate you, Target. Because the flip side of that shiny red bull's-eye coin is that you can't go in for one or two items. It's so easy to get distracted in the world of "what my house could look like" or "what I could dress like" that even though you only need lotion and tube socks for the eight-year-old, five minutes in you're thinking that you need to replace all of your glassware and you keep putting the beautifully decorated, trendy chevron Crock-pot in and out of your cart. And $171.58 later, as you walk out, you realize you forgot the tube socks. But you'll come back because you always do.

I Don't Understand Your Complete Commitment and Obsession to Become a Kitten.

My daughter Margaret loves animals. I cannot stress enough how much of an understatement that is. Her obsession with little animals is cute but always a little disconcerting to me. I am allergic to cats. I also don't like animals.

When she was about two, she decided she wanted to BE a kitten and acted like one and would only answer to her kitten name, "Pickles," not Margaret. This lasted for two and a half years. Her commitment to her new identity was impressive. She would insist on lapping up milk in bowls on the floor, eating dry cereal, which she meow-spoke was called "cat food," and if the doorbell would ring or we would scold her for something, she would scurry under the side table in the living room to hide.

Now, I knew my kids would have interests that weren't the same as mine, and I knew I'd have to find common ground on some of their life passions, especially if I didn't know much about those passions, but it really shocked me that she hasn't grown out of her commitment to BE an animal. I didn't see that coming, and I still don't like animals. Her love of them hasn't softened my cold, hard heart. Just the other day, at six years old, she said, "I wish I could yawn like a little kitten and have cute little claws!" When we talk about the future, she says, "I wish I could be a cat and live in your house and be YOUR cat and that you weren't allergic to cats!" She probably tells me once a week how much she wishes I wasn't allergic to cats. We have a house full of those creepy mechanical stuffed animals that make noise and move, but it's not good enough for her. (And, late at night, when the batteries are running low in those suckers and she rolls over on one in her sleep, it sends shivers down my spine.) I know her pleas should make me feel guilty, but I'm just relieved I have a legitimate reason to not buy a cute, fuzzy little animal that I would just resent and clean up after. (Please don't tell her about hairless cats, allergen-free cats, or shots to curb my allergies. I'm NOT INTERESTED.)

Side Rant

I don't get what people get out of the whole "pet situation." You pay for animals to get groomed, get them shots, buy them food, walk them or talk to them (?), and clean up after them. (I can't even think about cleaning up animal hair. I can't.) And in return you get what? They love you? They look up when you come home? I don't get it. That doesn't feel like a mutually beneficial relationship. I have friends and family members to talk to who love me and seem moderately happy to see me. So when people talk about their pets like they are humans, I'm genuinely confused. I don't say all of this as a point of pride, either. I actually think there's something wrong with me because I don't like animals, especially cute little kittens and bunnies.

127

Why Doesn't Everyone Realize My Child Is a Special Snowflake?

Not everyone is going to like your kids. I don't like that this shocked me, and I don't like that it's a thing. It's a horrible thought to hold your newborn and think, "Someday someone is going to be really mean to you." I hate everything about that thought. I expected fielding some dislike from kids because kids have unsophisticated tastes and their brains aren't fully developed, but when an adult doesn't like your kid, it's maddening. I know kids can be annoying, and I know the specific ways my own kids can be annoying, but of course I don't think their individual bags of weirdness are anything to hold against them. They're my special little snowflakes, after all!

One of my sons had a difficult teacher one year. She was part of a team-teaching class, so he only had her half of the day, but when we'd meet for parent-teacher conferences, she did all the talking. She gave us a lot of information on what he needed to work on, things he hadn't been criticized for before, and she insisted he be tested for learning disabilities and stress. He had started cracking his knuckles in class, for example, and it became apparent that he really just bugged her. We talked with our son about personality clashes and gave him a stress ball to squeeze in class, and he was oblivious to most of the criticism, BUT I WAS NOT. I had taught school before, and I know that teachers just want to help, so I listened to this teacher and tried to keep an open mind. I had my son tested and he was fine (better than "fine," actually). I brought the test results to her, and I laid my cards on the table and told her that the reason he had started cracking his knuckles in class was because he *was* stressed—and she was the one stressing him out. And she agreed. The rest of the year went okay. Did she learn to love him? I don't know. He wasn't ever her favorite, but he learned from her. We both did.

Don't Let Your Kids Know about Whole Milk Unless You're Prepared to Buy It All the Time Because There's No Going Back to Skim after That First Drop of Whole.

I was excited to be the kind of mom who exposed my kids to all the great opportunities in life—music, art, sciences, travel—but I was shocked by the number of opportunities they would be greedy for. I never imagined I would have to learn to say no in so many creative ways. (My favorite ways to say no are: "We'll see . . ." "Let's think about it, and if you still REALLY WANT TO DO IT in a week, then we'll see . . ." and "Wow. That sounds so cool. Too bad we can't do everything!")

In regards to our kids' schedules, my friend Kacy and I commit to what we've committed to, but we don't go into any commitment lightly. The same week my son said, "Hey, Mom, did you know kids can take karate?," Kacy's daughter said, "Mom, did you know there's this thing called 'dance class'?" We both replied the same way: "Huh. Never heard of it. Weird." That was our automatic coping mechanism because we know the difference between when kids are asking a question out of curiosity and when they're asking because it's their life's calling. We know when a kid really wants to take karate and when a kid will whine that he's too tired to go to karate a week and a half later when it's your turn to drive carpool.

Once your husband accidentally brings home whole milk after you have carefully conditioned the children to accept skim milk, well, there's no going back after that, either. Once you bribe your kids with Popsicles to clean up the yard, they're going to expect Popsicles from then on. You may not give in every time, but they will expect it. They will learn about iPhones, Disneyland, Chuck E. Cheese, sugared cereal, and all of life's indulgences even if you don't want them to know about them. I'm not saying these things are bad; I was just shocked that once you introduce something, there's no going back. They won't remember to make their beds even though you've reminded them every day for ten years, but they'll remember the exact day their older sister got her ears pierced and how old their older brother was when he got a cell phone. And even though each kid is different and has different needs, they will expect you to be "fair," which is the word they use when they want you to meet their expectations.

Since Nobody Asked: The Lisa Valentine Clark Story

Or, Advice that no one has requested, but that I desperately want to give

One thing I've learned from those Internet articles people post on Facebook is that birth order can predict your personality. So, pretty much the whole Internet says that as the oldest female in my family, I have the birthright to give advice. Apparently my siblings haven't read the same studies, because they don't want my advice. Weird. And I don't have a lot of followers as a blogger or on Facebook or anything, so, in an official capacity, I guess the Internet "doesn't care." Anywhoo, just because no one wants my advice, and just because I've already gone on the record in this very book that too many people are offering up advice, doesn't mean I can't just risk being a little hypocritical by giving a bit of advice in this book. It's been hard to restrain myself, but I want to keep it to a minimum. This is what I came up with:

Ignore the impulse for justice and fairness. You're not a cowboy. (If you are, this doesn't apply to you—carry on.) Life is inherently not fair. Sometimes that swings in your favor.

Just make the bed. Don't think about it, worry about

if you should or who should or how to do it. Just do it and move on with your day.

Be nice. Never suppress a generous thought (thank you, Bonnie Parkin). No act of kindness, no matter how small, is ever wasted (thank you, Aesop). Good manners are worth it.

Don't send that email without sleeping on it first. Ask a trusted adult for help. You know the email I'm talking about (don't pretend you don't).

Don't put a top sheet on your kids' beds. A fitted sheet and comforter are all they need, and omitting the top sheet will save you time and sanity (thank you, Kacy Faulconer).

No put-downs. This is a safe place. My parents had a sign with this motto on it in our home growing up. It's pretty straightforward—no put-downs, which means no belittling or being mean. And no swearing (thank you, Mom and Dad).

Pick up everything off the floor twice a day in less than five minutes. You can throw it away, put it away, or put it in a big box in the middle of your room. It doesn't matter. Just get it up off the floor.

Don't take yourself too seriously. Your kids don't.

Have Your Acceptance Speech Ready

There will come a day when you've had it. You want to make your point, and you need to be heard. You can accept the situation, or you can hope that the situation can be changed with some persistence and a carefully crafted speech. Here are some of my favorite speeches that I give on a regular basis:

1. I'm not the maid speech.

2. We don't live this way speech (otherwise known as the Don't leave your junk all over the lawn speech).

3. Grades are based on your ability to follow directions, not intelligence speech.

4. Why a college degree is necessary in today's job market/ global economy speech.

5. You need to be in charge of yourself speech.

6. One day your dad and I will be gone and all you'll have is your siblings speech.

7. We're paying for these lessons, the least you can do is practice speech.

8. One day your metabolism will slow down so set good habits now speech (otherwise known as the You can't live off Doritos and Pizza Pockets forever speech).

9. I didn't ask you who "did it," I just asked you to clean up that mess speech.

10. Don't lose your stuff speech (otherwise known as There's a place for everything so take the time to put it away speech).

It's About Focus, Not Balance

Or, Don't sing "Cat's in the Cradle"
while you're trying to work, or check your phone
while you're trying to talk to your kids

I prefer the word *focus* to *balance*. Everyone talks and writes about finding a good balance in life, and that rubs me the wrong way because there have been too many chunks of my life that had to be unbalanced in order to work, and no one is accounting for that. When I had a newborn, there was no "balance" in meeting everyone's needs, especially my own. You can't explain your emotional or physical needs to a baby. Can you imagine? *Hey, baby, stop crying, I really need to finish my writing project and then do some yoga, for my physical and emotional health. Do you understand my concern? You gonna help me out with this?* But that's okay. Stressing over whether I had time to exercise or do creative projects wasn't going to help anything. I was focused on falling in love with my new little person, meeting his or her every need, and using that time to think and desperately grab as much sleep as I possibly could. I don't regret the time that took or think back wistfully, wishing I'd had more time to lunch with friends or write interesting personal essays. In fact, I'm fiercely loyal to my old self, who was deep in the thick of keeping small humans alive in that new-born-to-five-years-old stage.

Now that I don't have anyone in that stage anymore, I have time to go to the gym, which is something new for me. And I do it not only to stay in shape but to gain muscle so I can—literally—lift heavy things and run around meeting older kids' needs all day without crumbling into an exhausted coma day in and out. But, truth be told, I exercise mostly to ward off anxiety about the things I worry about now that I have older kids and *I'm* older. I don't look at the women who bring babies and toddlers to the gym and think, *Oh, man, I totally should have done that. I should have gone earlier because now I feeeeeeelll so good.* I'm loyal to who I was, and I think, *Good for that girl who can do that. I would have rather clawed my eyes out with a melon baller than gotten a baby and two toddlers ready and out the door to the gym. It would have killed me. It would have sent me into a shame spiral.* And I laugh, because it would have.

One thing (yeah, just the one) that I had a really difficult time with, and still see no solution to, was the sleep issue in mothering. That bone-tired, never enough, rarely uninterrupted, lengthy, weary time without consistent, expected, lovely, R.E.M. sleep. I didn't sleep well when I was pregnant. I was huge and uncomfortable. I had heartburn and sciatica and a perpetually stuffy head. I nursed my newborns, and so they ate frequently. I did sleep training. But these things take time. In addition, factoring in other children and illness and Daylight Savings Time and all the random times they sleepwalk or have nightmares or whatever, and the fact that the probability of getting a good night's rest decreases exponentially with each child, it meant years of being tired. I had my kids close together—two or three years apart—which meant that I didn't really have a reserve of "catching up" (Ha! This is a lie! You don't ever "catch up!") on sleep. So I have roughly estimated that I went a good eleven or twelve years being really tired. Again, I'm not sure how I could have handled this issue better. Sleep is my Achilles' heel.

During this time, I wrote some really earnest, horrible poetry. It was an epic ode, written in the style of William Wordsworth. Like *Leaves of Grass.* I wanted to list the tiniest details of sleep that I most loved and missed, to express my desire for it to return to me, like a jilted lover who had gone away. There was a part about even *doctors who are on call get to sleep,* and on and on. I know it sounds ridiculous, but at the time *it wasn't a joke.* I wish I could find it to share here, but I probably ritualistically burned it in a beautiful dreamlike protest after a considerably long week of catnapping sleep. I scribbled it out in a notebook where I had intended to record cute things my kids said or did, and it is stained with tears. It is what desperate looks like. Desperation in physical form.

Soon after writing that horrible poem—which was over five pages long, some of it illegible scribbles—I made a promise to myself that ON THE DAY all my children go to school full-time, on that very first day of school, I will kiss them and send them on their way and then GO BACK TO BED and sleep for as long as I want. And not feel guilty. Somehow making that promise to myself gave me the perspective I needed to get through that time because I knew that day would come—or I hoped it would with so much fervor that it became real to me. I shifted my focus to looking ahead to the goal of blissful sleep while still retaining my love of late-night feedings and cuddling scared kids. The day hasn't come yet, but I'm really close AND I have been sleeping through the night consistently for three years now, so I'm a whole new person. I don't need to fulfill that promise because I actually feel like myself again, BUT I WILL DO IT because I still feel so bad for myself and because I promised myself. And so I will sleep, and I won't feel guilty.

Reflecting on different focuses in my life gives me hints on how to be authentic and gain a healthy life perspective. In those earlier years, I was happy. I didn't feel rushed, but I always felt tired, and it changed me. My idea of the best birthday or anniversary present back then would have included a decadent meal I didn't have to make and a NAP. Actually, it would have been a nap, then a really good meal, then an uninterrupted night's sleep, then a good brunch, and THEN a nap. Yes, sleep deprivation created a lot of bad, hastily written poetry, and that's just unfortunate, but when I think back about how I could have changed that, I realize that I did the best I could and it is what it is. It was a sacrifice, and there was no way I could have changed it and been the kind of mom I wanted to be—I CHOSE to be. There's satisfaction in that. I wasn't put upon. I wasn't living up to unrealistic expectations from anyone other than me—I did it my way. And I own that.

Our lives are constantly changing as our kids change, as our jobs change, as life circumstances and focus change. If we don't take the time to be reflective, we can't figure out what it is we like, what's working and what's not. We can get caught in a rut and miss opportunities or chances that could bless our lives. As Ferris Bueller warned us children of the '80s: "Life moves pretty fast. If you don't stop and look around once in a while, you could miss it." We have to take time to think, to evaluate and reevaluate what we've focused on and then find the energy to change and adapt—and sleep.

I sometimes have to risk looking like a slacker parent in order to be a really good one, the kind my particular kid needs me to be. Sometimes I have to, say, give up my pride and be late, miss meetings, seem distracted (actually BE distracted), or volunteer for less, or work more, or work less, or pick up my kids from school in sweaty gym clothes, or call it a day and cancel the errands to stay home and make popcorn, or go back to work, or quit a job, in order to meet my kids' needs.

Knowing what to do, and when, is the real test. Once I got overconfident and thought I had it all together for a minute. It was parent-teacher conferences, fall 2006. I had four kids and we were all there, dressed and hair combed and everything, and I was talking with my friend Cheri, whom I hadn't seen for a while, and we were catching up. Her calm, well-behaved children were older than mine, and she was teasing me about watching me across the street with all the hordes of kids coming in and out of my yard, relieved that it wasn't her. I feigned offense and with over-confidence told her emphatically that it wasn't chaos at my house, that everything was calm and together, *thank-youverymuch!* As if on cue, toddler Hugh immediately ran past us with his diaper down around his ankles, with Owen chasing him, yelling at him to come back! Cheri said something like, "Yeah, if you say so . . . ," wished me well, and went on her way. And that was the end of my confidence streak. I wish that were the only example I could think of, but I've seen myself through others' eyes enough to know that sometimes it does look like chaos. That's not necessarily a bad thing, it's just a by-product of having a bunch of kids. Once I let go of others' expectations and, most of all, my own expectations regarding ALL the good things I should or could be doing, ALL that I need to do is simplified. I need to have the courage to recognize that I don't know what I'm doing and I don't have it all together. Not only because I really don't have it all together. I'm not sure it's even possible to put everything together at the same time.

Sometimes I confuse the illusion of progress (getting things done, checking things off my list) with what I really want: IMPACT. Focus, by definition, can't be split. I hope that the accumulation of what I accomplish in any given day makes a difference, but the impact that I'm really looking for happens at unusual times and is hard to predict. It might be a good conversation with my teenager about his life goals while I'm making dinner or driving him to a music lesson. It might be just being there at the right time when my daughter experiences the drama of mean girls and has questions about navigating through that minefield. It could be talking about the sounds each letter makes on the walk back from kindergarten. Or maybe a "good night" from one of my kids will turn into a late-night talk about more pressing, personal questions. It could be taking time to have fun, too, like playing a game (I hate board games, but kids love them, it's a thing), or sitting and painting with my kids, or taking them out for a treat just because they need it. You never know what will have an impact, which conversation will make its mark and get the coveted place in the long-term-memory hall of fame in their brains.

Splitting our focus to get all the things done that we need to get done seems to be part of the parenting package. At the risk of sounding like a martyr, I will state with unemotional exactness that I don't think I do anything anymore without interruption. Folding laundry and answering questions, making dinner and managing homework, taking a shower and fielding requests, it's the bundle package I signed up for without reading the fine print when welcoming kids into my home. If I can't find my children, or the house seems too quiet, all I have to do is get on the phone, and that will bring everyone running to me. And, for the most part, I can handle it, but we all have our limits. When my kids laugh at me as I space off, unable to finish a sentence, or I forget where I put my cell phone and they laugh because it's right there in my hand, sure, "it's funny," but it's their fault. My brain is split because they have conditioned it to be that way through years of ~~torture~~ training. So, laugh it up, kids, you broke Mom.

Focusing on one task at a time is becoming a lost art, like letter writing and such courting rituals as gifting locks of hair. (I actually once had a boyfriend give me a severed dreadlock as a gift when we were dating. Years later my husband and I found it in an old box and it freaked us out because we thought it was a rat so we quickly threw it away. I guess some lost arts are better left dead.) As a proud multitasker, I haven't always found it easy to slow down and focus on really listening to my kids. When chubby little toddler hands physically pull your face toward them so that you will really listen to them, well, that's a good reminder. I hate it when I'm talking to someone and they're looking at their phone through the whole conversation. It feels like a slight. I like undivided attention, and my kids are no different, so I try to be present and physically look at them when they're talking to me, even if it means I need to stop what I'm doing. And if I can't stop at that moment, then setting aside time for them later sends the message that I want to listen to them and talk with them.

When I was writing and filming the web series *Pretty Darn Funny,* the other producers I worked with, Jeff Parkin and Jared Cardon, were very encouraging of the focus I have. They regularly met at my convenience—at my house, most of the time with kids coming in and out—as we wrote and shot the series. The other writers, Kacy, Adrienne, and Tom, needed the same considerations, so it worked out really well. We consolidated our shooting schedule to save money and to protect ourselves from long periods of time away from our families. Putting together the series was a lot of work, but it was only a few crazy days, with reasonable hours the rest of the time. This was an ideal situation, and because we were creating our own job, we had the control to make our own model.

Just because something has always been done a certain way doesn't mean it has to be done that way. If enough of us are willing to encourage a more flexible workplace in other fields and in our culture in general, it could change the workforce model, which could benefit families in a major way. Every article or discussion I read or take part in seems to point to a future in which work follows this flexible-but-focused-chunks-of-time model as opposed to a traditional 9 to 5 model. If any group knows how to implement this kind of new workforce model, it's the adaptable moms, who have been dealing with a larger number of things to focus on than any other group. I like that flexibility, and although I realize that not all jobs can be that flexible, some of them can. And in our own homes, certainly the way we mother can be flexible, and what our family focus is and how we focus our mind, heart, and attention can be.

Sitting down to write this book showed me how flexible I've become in adjusting to everyone's changing needs (good for me!), but it has also made me reevaluate how available I am. Too available. My children are not babies anymore, they're all kids. They can learn more patience. They can learn more respect for others' time and priorities. And I can teach them those things by showing them I'm working on something. They can wait to use the computer, or respect some time I need. THEY can adjust, too *(good for them)!* So if I repeat myself in this book, this is my official excuse: I'm fragmented 'cause my kids broke my brain. The other day my son called me from middle school in the middle of the day, and this is how the conversation went:

Owen: Hey, Mom.

Me: Hey, Owen. Everything all right? What's going on?

Owen: My tooth came out.

Me: You lost your tooth?

Owen: Yeah.

Me: Oh, wow. Okay. [He's fourteen, and so I'm pretty sure this is his last baby tooth. He sounded bored on the phone, too.]

Owen: Well, yeah.

pause

Me: Well, uh, way to go. Is there a reason you called?

143

Owen: Well, yeah, will you come and pick up my tooth?

Me (*surprised*): Why?

Owen: Uh, you know, for the tooth fairy or whatever.

Me (*laughing*): Oh yeah, well, I think the jig is up on that one! Just bring it home if you want; I don't need to come and get it.

Owen: But I don't have a pocket.

Me: Just put it in some tissue or, better yet, just throw it away. You know I don't have a box of your baby teeth in my sock drawer or anything, right? We don't keep them. That's creepy.

Owen: But I don't have a pocket.

Me: So, lemme get this straight. You want me to drive to the middle school and pick up your baby tooth because you don't have a pocket?

Owen: Well, yeah.

Me (*laughing*): Yeah, I'm not doing that. Have a great day!

I haven't found any secret to finding a good balance to all the things I want to do in life, so I don't really think about my life in terms of balance anymore. Being a mother means everything to me. I know that's not the way everyone feels, but that's how I feel. I've always wanted to be a mom. I wanted to do a lot of other things, too, but I didn't grow up thinking being a mom would exclude me from those other things. I know it seems nerdy to say "I love being a mom!" and it's not very progressive or new or shocking, but I don't really care. It's what I think. And that has everything to do with my kids and not me, and I get that. So, even though I can't separate my life into little compartments containing all the things I want to do, because they all bleed into each other, I try to focus on each task. When I'm talking with my kids, I'm not on the phone. When I'm working, I'm focusing on doing a good job. And I do what needs to be done first.

I recognize that most of us don't mother our kids under perfect circumstances, but I do believe most of us get to choose what kind of moms we'll be amid circumstances blissful and difficult and everything in between. And so, with all that I read and say about balancing career goals and family life, balancing money and hobbies, balancing needs and wants, and balancing the individual and the family, I see that there are few easy answers or formulas. I'm careful not to judge other moms' choices because nothing brings me more hurt or anger than when I feel I'm being judged as a mother. It's the opposite of helpful. I'm consistently impressed with the way my mom friends are able to do what needs to be done, so I'm not concerned with trying to write a list of things to keep in mind when balancing x, y, and z. There are many good solutions, and they all require you to be *present*. Being a mom is, at its very best, fun, meaningful, and the most creative act I know. I don't want to forget the great joy in it because that's what I want to keep as my focus.

Raising human beings is no joke. Well, it *is* funny and

ridiculous, but it's serious business, too. These kids are the building blocks of societies. They are our future leaders, innovators, teachers, nurturers, policy makers, and comedic writers. They are the ones who will take care of us in our old age (this is where I start singing Harry Chapin's hit parental-guilt classic "Cat's in the Cradle"). We are shaping how they see the world and trying to give them a glimpse as to what the world *should* be like, too, not just what it actually is. These are high stakes, so I'm trying to be present and not distracted. I'm trying not to wish away this moment for the idea of another one. And that is harder to do than I thought. I guess that's the test.

Advice You Didn't Ask For

When preparing children for school, most parents push practicing ABCs, numbers, and shapes, which is great, but I also suggest you practice handing in papers with your children. Give them a piece of paper, have them scribble on it, and have them practice handing it back to you. When they have mastered that (if they do; no judgment if they don't), have the child take a piece of paper to a neighbor's house, have the neighbor scribble on it and hand it back to your child, and have the child hand it back to you. This is surprisingly difficult and the reason why junior high was created.

It Takes a Village, but Mostly a Mother (and That Village Is Full of Moms)

Or, Why would I want a piece of toast when I could have a Monte Cristo?

Every time I hear the comment "It takes a village . . ." in regards to how other people help raise our kids, I read it internally as a way for someone else to take credit for all the good parts that parents do in raising their kids, leaving the sludge at the bottom of the parenting cup to mothers. Like it's a team effort when they graduate from high school, but if the kid flunks out, then the team suddenly turns on the moms and asks *"Well, where are the parents?!"* I feel like an indignant Little Red Hen standing around with a warm loaf of bread and everyone is demanding a slice. Oh, is the village going to run out and get diapers for me at 11:00 at night? Register and pay for ballet lessons? Teach my kids how to be patient and have good table manners? Develop photos at Costco the night before the science fair project is due? Take their rectal temperature in the middle of the night? Oh, "the village" has it covered, does it?

I don't mean to diminish the role other key players have in the lives of our kids. Others have an influence on our kids in ways and at times when we can't, and we need those people—family members, extended family, close friends, mentors, heroes, teachers. Actually, I think these people are critical when raising kids. My mom and dad are more like second parents than extended family. They are always around for my kids, and they are helping us raise them in a real way—feeding them, showing up for recitals and ball games, talking with them about everything. They fill in the cracks of things I mean to talk to my kids about or things I have tried to address but my effort hasn't reached the inner workings of my kids' brains in the same way as it does when Grandma and Grandpa say it. They have a real connection that is sometimes threatening to me as a mom, to be honest. My kids like them more than they like me, but it's not a contest . . . (But if it were, it's not a fair one. I mean, to begin with, I can't give my kids gum every single time I see them!) When I do say that out loud, that my kids like them more than me, my parents both just laugh, but they never correct me. They just say something to the effect of we *all* have the same goal and we *all* just love these kids!

I don't want to diminish the small acts of kindness others do for us or for our kids, either. But that's not what I hear when I hear "It takes a village . . ." Because the day-in, day-out knowing of your kids' needs and wants and abilities and adjusting your day and budget and time to them is what you can't quantify. Moms do secret things nobody else sees that the village can't really do the way a mom can. These are secret because sometimes they are gross and deal with bodily fluids; they are secret because they are tedious and monotonous, but have to be done; and they are secret because they are special and private and hard to put into words. It's not that other people don't want to help or that they don't. I just don't appreciate even the subtle suggestion that we're all equally sharing the load. It doesn't ring true to me.

Men will regularly get congratulated for taking their kids to Costco by themselves or volunteering at school, but we just assume mothers should be doing all that. We would never consider congratulating a mom for, say, taking all the kids to the post office to run an errand. My friend Christian regularly takes his kids to the grocery store and is embarrassed by how many people stop him to tell him what a good dad he is for doing so. This is one of the reasons why we have all the "Oh, I'm JUST a mom" mentality. And then when moms DO say something to that effect: "I'm JUST a mom . . ." we berate them and tell them not to say that, and to take a little more pride in the calling, like, again, we need approval to do whatever we want and to feel however we want to feel about it. We can't win.

In this "village" of American culture, I've learned that most people don't see what you do day in and day out. That's okay, I guess. No one likes a show-off. You learn special, sacred things about your kids when you watch them, which has immeasurable power. You can literally be with them all of the time and still "miss" their growing up. Sometimes it does happen overnight, and you find yourself looking around for that cute blonde toddler who wore piggy tails and princess dress-ups and sang every day and you realize she's a sophisticated eleven-year-old who does back handsprings and speaks French. It's weird. I see it as a privilege, not just a duty, to spend as much time with my kids as possible and have whatever positive influence I can have on them. Now that I have an almost-sixteen-year-old, and I think of him leaving home in two years, it hits me in the gut and I don't like it. I will still encourage him to grow up, move on, and move out, because that's what I should do and it's what is best for him. But I don't see any other member of "the village" having as hard a time thinking about it as I do.

I don't want to sound like a martyr. Topher is a great parenting partner and we make a really good team; I lucked out in choosing a man who turned out to be an incredible father. Maybe I should delegate more things and let some things go. I'm getting better at that. But when I evaluate the other moms I admire and their contributions, and I see what they've had to do and sometimes can't even talk about, I conclude that moms somehow do what needs to be done. And I like being part of that village.

I don't know if I could do what I have to do, especially as a mom, without my friends. I think one of my greatest accomplishments in life is choosing the very best friends. I could write a chapter about each one of them. I have a handful of friends whom I would drop anything for if they called, and they'd do the same for me. Everyone should have a few friends like that. I've heard a lot of moms say they don't have time for friends. I get what they mean over-all—you have less time to nurture friendships when you're raising kids—but this line of thinking always makes me feel so uncomfortable. Moms need friends because if this really is the most important work we can do in life, then we have to do our very best, and doing our best means calling in for reinforcements. And, bonus: This is the village we get to handpick!

My little network, my chosen village, is pretty diverse. I have friends who are invaluable to me because they're a little further along the parenting road than I am and they prepare me for what's ahead. Like my cousin Julie, who told me about the pitfalls of the Eagle Scouting paperwork, and how when your son leaves on a mission and you prepare to say good-bye to him and not see him for two years, "it's worse than you think, but no one tells you." But *she* did. I also have friends who don't have kids, friends who are new moms, and friends who have different parenting strengths or philosophies from mine. Our connection is just friendship, not motherhood, even though they all support me in that role.

These are the kind of friends who don't keep score or hold grudges. They understand that I'm putting my family first and so I need to be flexible when making plans, but I'm so excited and energized when I do talk to them or see them. They know what I'm doing and urge me on— often because they're doing similar things, or if they're not, they value what I'm doing and help me not take myself too seriously. They are loyal to me and also to my husband, and they give him the benefit of the doubt the way they do me because they want to support my marriage, too. I need them because sometimes motherhood is lonely and isolating, and having a connection, however small, can be a lifeline. I can say things to them I can't say to my kids. I can check myself (as I should, before I wreck myself) with this trusted village of friends.

When I found out I was having a second boy, I realized that, as a former girl, I didn't know much about raising boys, and I should read up. My research led me to the book *The Wonder of Boys* by Michael Gurian and the idea of the "second family." We parents are the first family, but the second family is the extended family, community, or tribe. In the book, Gurian quotes Kurt Vonnegut Jr. as saying:

"Until recent times, human beings usually had a permanent community of relatives. They had dozens of homes to go to. So when a married couple had a fight, one or the other could go to a house three doors down and stay with a close relative until he or she was feeling tender again. Or if the kids got so fed up with their parents that they couldn't stand it, they could march over to their uncle's for a while.

"Now this is rarely possible. Each family is locked into its little box. The neighbors aren't relatives. There aren't other houses where people can go and be cared for. When we ponder what's happening to America—'Where have all the values gone?' and all that—the answer is perfectly simple. We're lonesome. We don't have enough friends or relatives any more. And we would if we lived in real communities."

Gurian calls for "an openness to nonblood 'relations.'

Though we Americans are trained to do everything individualistically, we must come to realize that once we have kids, individualism is impractical and self-defeating. The myth that 'all my boy needs is me,' is just that—a myth." If I sometimes think I'm too busy for friends and I need to simplify and focus on just my kids, it's not only me who is missing out.

I have seen these kinds of second-family relationships pay off in real ways for me. I grew up in Lincoln, Nebraska, away from all extended family, but my friends' moms and also my parents' close friends were part of our "second family" and had a huge impact on me. I watched Jill and Nancy and spent a lot of time in their homes talking to them. I always felt like I was special to them, and they are still special to me. When they talked about families or the gospel or life choices, I paid close attention. They have influenced the way I raise my kids.

Topher and I have tried to create these kinds of relationships for our kids, and I know that our kids look up to our friends. These are friends who have taken the time to talk with my kids and tease them and have their own meaningful relationships with them. They are friends with whom my sons can laugh at their parents' expense in a safe way. Like when my older boys say they're rebelling by going into science and technology fields and not the arts like their parents, or when our daughter was so obsessed with animals that she wouldn't answer to her given name, only her cat name, "Pickles," for two years and I don't like animals.

My kids need mentors who know them and love them and want to help me raise them. I didn't think I would need to know about coding or graphic design or veterinary science to connect with my kids, but here I am, and here enters the second family. And it feels so great, like an honor, when a kid who isn't yours but whom you have loved for his or her entire life comes to you and wants to ask you questions about studying Shakespeare, painting, or dating.

When my kids need real advice about important things like faith, careers, relationships, and decision making, they already know what their parents think. So it's nice to know they have a small group of trusted adults who are invested in them and know what's at stake in ways that I can't because I'm a different person. My friends reinforce the values that I'm teaching my kids, and they live full, happy lives in different ways than Topher and I have, which shows the kids that there are different ways to live well. I think that is crucial for kids as they are finding their own paths.

And I will gladly share a healthy portion of my warm loaf of bread with this group. If I can be completely obnoxious about this Little Red Hen metaphor and just keep going with it, not only am I sharing that slice of bread, but my second family would totally bring smoked meats, fancy cheeses, and perhaps an exotic mango chutney to the table as well. And they would probably deep-fry it, too. And why would I want a piece of toast when I could have a Monte Cristo?

More Advice You Didn't Ask For

Hoard food for yourself. Kids will eat everything good first and leave nothing for you. Think ahead and always have a treat on hand. I won't insult you by even suggesting what that treat should be. You know. Before I had kids, a friend I worked with told me about a time she climbed on top of the refrigerator to eat a cookie by herself while her young children cried and tried to claw at her in order to get at the cookie. Apparently she called her mom and was crying as she was eating this cookie . . . on top of the refrigerator. When I heard this story I was horrified; I thought it was so bizarre and kinda mean. Twenty years later, I think, *I hope it was a good cookie and not some packaged generic junk.*

I'm So Busy, I'm Surprised I Had Time to Write This!

Or, What am I up to? Oh, stuff and things

Being busy seems to have become a virtue, so much that we brag about it. "Oh, I'd love to sit down and read a book, but I am SO BUSY with the PTA Extravaganza I just don't have a moment to spare!" "Oh, I WISH I could volunteer at the school. I'm launching my new website for underprivileged owls today and I'm so swamped!" and so on. We don't have After School Specials on TV anymore, but if we did, there wouldn't be any episodes about how to help kids to become busier. This is not something that we consciously aspire to, although it is something that we have unknowingly created. "BUSY" isn't a virtue. It's not in the Young Women Value rainbow of colors, but if it did have a color, I imagine it would be black, signifying a black hole of nothingness.

It's a common theme among women of different ages, backgrounds, and stages of life: EVERYONE is really busy. Every woman I know feels overwhelmed about one or more aspects of her life. Even women who are deliberate and organized. Even moms who simplify their kids' activities or try to cut out unnecessary stresses. I think it has a lot to do with how we structure our lives and what we value. If you are trying to live a Christlike life of service and to teach that way of life to your kids, for example, you have a lot of responsibilities and could really "just" do THAT (be an active member of the Church) and find most of your nights full. If you work full-time, you are meeting the needs of your family *and* your job, which is meeting the needs of a company or organization or a group of other people's needs. And most of us are trying to manage our expectations of what we *should be* accomplishing during a day while facing the reality of what we *really are able* to accomplish. After all, our lives are not neatly compartmentalized into manageable bites: work, family, hobbies, interests, volunteering, emergencies, home management, friends, and so on. These areas of our lives all bleed together. We are asked to do a lot of *stuff.* We can choose what we do, and we should own those choices, but we need to be aware that a lot is asked of US ALL. Let's just acknowledge that.

Of course, knowing this should help us be sensitive to the amount of time and tasks we request from others. But instead I think it makes us try to validate ourselves to others by listing off all the reasons why we're so busy, like it's some sort of twisted competition of misery.

I get sick of people saying "simplify your life," especially in terms of motherhood, because you can't *have* five kids and simplify your life. If I lived alone and could actually choose to do ONE THING, maybe it would be simple. But I chose to have a lot of kids, and I have to own that choice. I have a lot of energy and drive, and I'm up for it (most days). But simplification doesn't involve our choices alone. We also have things to manage, like cell phones, cars, Internet service, insurance for everything, toys, books, clothes for everyone, cleaning supplies, socks, Legos, homework, bills, and one million other things, and those "things" take time, consideration, money, and thought. It's a lot to think about.

So, brass tacks, what are we doing with our twenty-four hours every day? In my own family, Church-wise, if you list it out, we study the scriptures, have family prayer and family home evening, and are involved in seminary, Cub Scouts, activity days, Primary, the Scouting program (campouts and powwows and merit badges), Young Men activities, Relief Society, bishopric meetings, and home teaching and visiting teaching. It's a list! And even if you do only one thing for each auxiliary, it's still a lot of things. It's the same with the kids' extracurricular activities and education. Even if each of your kids chooses just one thing to do, or two things, like a music lesson and one sport, that's a lot of "things" to think about, drive to, pay for, talk about, plan, invest in, attend, and everything. And I haven't even talked about grades or social engagements.

When I read through my journal, I see that there are different kinds of "busy." *What did you do today?* is an innocent enough question, but when I had a lot of small children it seemed that I was always doing something but rarely accomplishing anything—in my mind, anyway. I would answer that question with "I don't know, but I'm exhausted. I think I wiped down the fridge a couple of times, and I put on little shoes and we walked and read, and I wanted to finish the laundry but I forgot to change the load, but we looked at a caterpillar for a long time, or . . . something else?"

It's not like I didn't have a list in my head about what I wanted to accomplish. I don't know what my problem is, but I always think I can accomplish about five more projects on any given day than I really can. And with a baby or a potty-training toddler, one errand is all you can manage at one time without factoring in the time and energy for an unexpected meltdown. (I've nursed and changed a baby in my minivan in the parking lot of Walmart more than once. I know things. This was a primitive time in child rearing, before Amazon Prime delivered everything you might need. We managed, and we did it by elaborate planning and tim-ings of feedings/changings/parking next to a cart to load the sleeping baby and drop the toddler in the basket/list ready/snacks ready/time of day perfectly organized. Or we just went to the store when the kids were in bed. If you want to see a bunch of moms walk aimlessly around, go to Target at about nine p.m. I used to see all my friends there. It's great. Grab a bag of Dove chocolates and be on your way.) But productive mothering isn't something we spend a lot of time talking about, measurable or not.

Being busy and being productive are different things. My father, for example, loves to be busy. He can't sit still. He is in his seventies, but the thought of retiring seems outrageous to him. "What am I going to do, sit around? Play golf? Can you imagine!? Ugh, it's so boring!" He claims to have adult ADD, which he probably does, but he's really productive. He feels passionately about things and he's busy doing them. He works for a university, reads voraciously, serves the community, posts really impassioned articles on Facebook, and cleans out the kitchens in church buildings across the stake (I'm not sure if that's his official calling, but it's clearly his "calling," you know?), and he has always been this way. My mother is no different. She is past retirement age and still works full-time in education doing a million things with publishing and mentoring, and she teaches her grandkids sketching and painting and is currently a stake Relief Society president. It's a little ridiculous when I think of criticizing being busy to not mention that I find my parents very admirable in the way they spend their time and contribute to their families and community in specific ways. They're not sitting around waiting for life to happen or relaxing and enjoying any time off. As my brother-in-law Will said with great accuracy, "Your parents don't know they're old!" They don't; no one told them. My mother told her Laurel class that once they entered Relief Society, "We're all the same age!" And she believes it. There's no slowing down Bob and Shauna.

This was the environment in which I was raised: Do your best, but go out there and do—don't sit around doing nothing. Be productive. Don't waste time. Don't decide if you're going to make your bed or not, just do it.

Don't decide whether or not you're going to go to college, of course you are, so go do it and don't waste your time by getting bad grades, just do it. If you're going to read a book or watch TV (valued activities in my family) or go to a movie (our favorite), then do it. You need downtime to recharge and meditate, too, so do it. But take opportunities and get involved in doing what you love.

My husband, Topher, is the busiest person I know, but he doesn't talk about it. I've learned a lot about what it means to be productive on your own terms by watching him. I have never known him to have fewer than two jobs at a time. In graduate school he was the only student who had kids and a job and a church calling. He worried that the other students had time to sit in the pub and discuss and study more than he had time to, but it turned out it wasn't a disadvantage after all. He did very well and earned the scholarship offered that year due to his great work. I'm very proud of all Topher has accomplished, but mostly because he is careful with his time. Though he has always had more than one job, he schedules downtime. He always has to have something to look forward to—a date night, getting together with friends, or a creative project— to get him through. He's not conflicted about setting aside time to read a book or go to a movie because he feels he's deserved it. He regularly rewards himself for working hard. He's not tormented by indecision, he just puts everything down on a schedule and it works for him. It's actually been really great for our family because he prioritizes his responsibilities in a measurable way.

Topher's system has been a good example to me to prioritize what I need to do, but I feel much more conflicted about my responsibilities than he does because they are not always measurable. I feel very strongly about the responsibility we women have to our ancestor mothers because of our increased opportunities. I tell my girls that never in the history of the world have they had more opportunities and blessings available to them as women. There are so many ways for women to contribute to something good out there—ways that haven't always been available. My daughters are able to take this reality for granted, and I think it's exciting. This is the way life should be. We should have all of the opportunities open to us and use those opportunities to do great things for ourselves, our families, and the world. I get really caught up in that idea.

Of course, as with all things, there are inherent traps and unique problems with having so many good choices. But I don't want that to rob my daughters of the joy and excitement they have laid out before them. I know that they will feel a lot of pressure to do more and be more with families and careers, and that it will be really intense, so I want them to know about the beauty and simplicity of happiness at the same time they pursue all the good things they want. I don't want them to feel overwhelmed, which is often what I think of when I hear the word *busy*.

Some people make their busy-ness seem effortless, but

that only works in artificial, removed settings. Sometimes reading blogs is like reading a bunch of those braggy Christmas letters. Every day. But not all blogs are unrealistic. Some of them are self-deprecating, some "awesome" (a scientific term my husband and I use regularly to describe someone who tries so hard that it's difficult to look away, and all you want to do is put your arm around that person and say, "It's okay, it's okay. Calm down. We LIKE you!"), and some just matter-of-fact. But they all have an undeniable element to them: They invite readers into their perspective for a second, and it seems harmless, but they want something from you. I have read many blogs. I know several pretty well-known bloggers myself. I have a blog I never write on (because I'm SO BUSY—just kidding, I'm just doing something else). And what you read on blogs is not real. Not because you're being tricked or duped, but because no one can present his or her full life, with the rich nuances of feelings, successes, failures, strengths, weaknesses, thoughts, and, most important, the sacred, small moments, the big life changes, effects of meditation, and personal conversations and daily decisions that make us who we are IN ONE BLOG! It's not possible! It's a small snippet in time diffused by the moment, the perspective AT THE TIME you read it, and filtered again by your own perspective and experience in that moment. It's not the full story.

If we don't want to do something, why can't we just say we don't want to do it? Why do we have to "prove" how busy we are in order to get out of it? In one of my favorite *Pretty Darn Funny* episodes, "Basket Case," there's a scene where my character, Gracie, gets into a contest of "who's the busiest" with her friend Charmin. The conversation escalates to the point where, in order to show up this other woman, Gracie has found herself agreeing to come up with thirty baskets for a PTA fund-raiser. The rest of the episode shows how she kills herself doing it and complaining about it all the way. The scene was one of my favorites to film (1) because I got to wear a drop-off dickey and (2) because one-upping about all the things we do to prove we're busy is such a thing. I'm trying to question my motives.

If our goal is to accomplish more than anyone else, what do we create with the accumulation of these frantic days? Our busyness makes us, who have so many demands, seem frantic, distracted, and silly—and for what? To win an imaginary contest? Or are we filling our time with *xyz* in order to avoid something else? Is it a pride thing—that we won't let anyone else do what only we can do? Is it a power play—that we control everyone's lives or programs or jobs? Is it for validation—"busy = important"?

I try not to say "I'm so busy!" but it's so hard because I *feel* busy. I feel like I'm moving around a lot of the day, and some days I think that's just the reality of my choices. It's also a short way to answer, "How are you? What have you been up to?" when you don't really know what to say. The reality of my situation is usually that I've said yes to a lot of things, and I want to fulfill my commitments, so this day is going to be packed. But not every day has to be like that. And a really busy day, when I don't have more than a minute or two to sit down, is a good day to remember that this is not my goal. It's not the ideal. I shouldn't be striving for this kind of life. There is value in sitting and thinking and not doing as much. It's a reminder for me that there is not extra value in appearing busy (or "appearing anything") to anyone. That's not a real thing, or at least not an attractive state of being. Being busy is not a contest. It's a cultural thing that is not helpful to anyone.

Having time to process and think, all while considering your own and other people's schedules, is the real underrated virtue. Many important tasks cannot be listed and checked off, but that doesn't diminish their importance. Even though I like to be productive, I can't measure my success as a mother by tasks accomplished. I want to stop everything when my kids need me, NOT to come pick them up from school because they don't want to walk three blocks home, NOT to run to the store because they want nachos and we don't have any shredded cheese, but when they *really* need me, like when they learn their best friend is moving and they need someone to listen, or when they're frustrated about school or changing friend dynamics and they need to talk it out. I want my kids to work hard and look for good opportunities to do great things, but I don't want them to get caught up in the trap of being so busy they don't have time to do what they love. And I don't want my friends to think I'm too busy for them, or my kids to think of me as too busy to enjoy life, because that is the opposite of how I want to live my life. So I won't identify myself as "busy," but it does seems a little arrogant to answer the question, "What are you up to?" with "Productive. I'm super productive right now!"

Maybe it's choice and accountability that is the underrated virtue. I'm trying to teach my kids to guard time so they have enough time to pray and ponder about the things that really matter, like who they want to be, what they want to accomplish in life, and how they can best help others. I want them to be careful to schedule time to learn, serve, and think outside of their own world. I want their minds to be searching for ways to be peaceful, deliberate, and loving to the world. But it seems pretty self-righteous to answer the question, "What are you up to?" with "Deliberate. I'm very deliberate in my life."

So if you ask me, "What are you up to?" I'll probably answer, "I don't know. Stuff?" and you'll know what I mean.

More Advice You Didn't Ask For
but if I Don't Give It, We'll All Regret It

Give yourself a day off. If you're running a household, your home is a constant reminder of what you need to do as well as the constant unraveling of all you do accomplish. And we both know that you will see this tip and read "day" but really only take off "an hour or two." Take one "day" to do whatever. You're on call 24/7, and even doctors have an on-call room at the hospital where they can sleep. When all the people who work 9 to 5 are kicking up their heels to watch TV and eat, that's your "GO!" time. And if you're working 9 to 5, that's even MORE reason to give yourself a mental slack day.

Side Rant

I get so irked when, on Mother's Day or Father's Day, one of my kids inevitably says something like, "Hey, when's Kids' Day?" with an indignant attitude, like they need to right some wrong and balance out the universe. Like we can't just have the one special day about parenting or somehow it will spoil us. I always reply, "Oh, that's every day. Kids' Day is like, a regular Tuesday. Choose any day. That's Kids' Day."

Don't resist the urge to celebrate your little victories. Not for the kids. No, they get enough awards, accolades, and attention for doing things.

I'm talking about the small victories that will have a huge impact on the quality of your life, like the time my sister-in-law Suze discovered she could vacuum linoleum and didn't have to sweep (a huge time saver!), or the time when my small children were sick and I discovered white, cherry-flavored Popsicles (a huge stain saver!), or just recently when I realized that eggs are a cheap, protein-filled food that can satisfy my teenage boys for at least one of their many daily meals (a huge budget and time saver!) Victories are victories.

What Is My Job, Exactly?

Or, My kids are not an extension of me and their choices are their own, but I would make really good choices for them, so what do I do with that?

Soon after I had my fifth child, my oldest, Miles, started coming into his own as a preteen. (This age is oddly fun because they start to assert their independence in the cutest ways. They have their own opinions and personal style, they want their hair a certain way, and they ask questions that require longer explanations.) I had a startling realization that I had known was true in theory, because it was logical and has been clearly documented historically in a lot of different publications, but it had been pushed out of my mind in the all-encompassing business of taking care of small children. Despite my best efforts at denial, this realization had sunk in slowly, as if my subconscious didn't want to accept it at first and eased me into it so as to not give me a heart attack. The realization was this: It doesn't really matter what I do or say because, at the end of the day, my kids' choices are their own and not mine. It is just disconcerting to know that no matter what I teach my kids—the gospel, the scriptures, the good literature, the prayers, the good habits, the example, the music, everything I want my kids to know and internalize—it doesn't matter because they get to make the final decision and most of the little decisions before that. It's on them.

"It doesn't really matter what I do or say" in that context means I could, theoretically, be the very best mother on the planet, and one of my kids could still choose something, or many things, that would go against what I want or what I think is good. They could even choose something horrible and painful. They are not an extension of me. They are not brainwashed. They have the freedom to break my heart, to hurt themselves, or to hurt others—and that's the way God intended it. That's part of the plan of happiness. The plan is for them to find their own way to listen to the Holy Ghost, make choices, develop their talents, gain experience, and ultimately return to God. After all we say and do, we just want our kids to be happy, and so we show them the way, we set a good example, we even plead. But then we have to let go.

Even when realizing all of this, isn't there a moment in every mother's life when, as dedicated a member of The Church of Jesus Christ of Latter-day Saints as she is, she thinks to herself, *But I love them more than they know. And I KNOW better.* As much as she has faith and hope and charity, she pauses for a moment and in that place thinks, *If they just followed me and did what I wanted them to do, then they'd be happier. Then we all would.* As much as she believes in agency, she thinks, *Just trust me. I can make good choices for you. Just do what I SAY.* Don't we all have that moment when we question why they won't (or why they shouldn't) just give up their will to ours? That's an uncomfortable space to live in. I can imagine my friend Stace, an emotionally in-tune mother of three and a life coach, saying just that, "Live in that space. What does that feel like?" It feels desperate and wrong, though well-intentioned.

Coming to this realization was a game-changing moment for me. Because I recognized that I have spent so much energy—how about ALL my energy?—raising these kids with the intent that my parenting would lead them to a happy, successful life, and now this realization made me wonder if that was possible at all. If not, then what was the point to anything I was doing? I regularly have panicked moments at odd times, flashes of unhelpful "what ifs" that go something like this:

- What if I'm the best mom and it's not enough for them?
- What if I'm not up to the task of all that they need?
- What if my kids grow up and hate the way I raised them?
- What if my kids become drug addicts or criminals? How will I help them?
- What if they never learn how to take care of themselves? Then what?

At the same time I "lived in this space," I thought about other moms I knew. Some of the very best moms I know have kids who have rejected Christ and His teachings, who don't believe in Christ but are good and kind people.

Others have kids who are not kind or good people. Some of the best moms I know have children who are addicts or who cannot take care of themselves. Others have children who have served Christlike lives amid a variety of circumstances. At the end of the day, most moms are mothering under conditions they didn't anticipate, with children who are all different than they thought they'd be. It seems to me that how our kids "turn out" doesn't measure our effectiveness as parents, but sometimes we try to convince ourselves that it does, or that it should.

I don't want to underestimate the importance of what we do as mothers. I really do believe it's the most important work I'll do in my life. I don't want to say, "It doesn't matter, so lighten up" on your responsibilities, insight, or whatever, as if the stakes weren't high. A lot of problems are eliminated, lessened, or lifted by good mothers. I believe, as Julie B. Beck has said, that "There is no limit to what a woman with a mother heart can accomplish. Righteous women have changed the course of history and will continue to do so, and their influence will spread and grow exponentially throughout the eternities." We just don't want to get it wrong. We just want our kids to be happy. What's the right balance between caring enough to recognize we can make all the difference and not fooling ourselves into thinking we have all the influence and control? Thinking we can control or should control all of the activities, thoughts, ideas, and actions of our children is counterintuitive to living the gospel, however well-intentioned. Our desire for more control in our children's lives sometimes comes out of fear—fear that we can't do enough or be enough or that we might make a mistake. Fear is frantic and not methodical and purposeful.

How your kids "turn out" (and when, exactly, does that happen? It's so arbitrary. Is it when they're eighteen, or in their late twenties? Do we "turn out" when we hit a certain age, or when we've reached a milestone or an accomplishment?) is not really a thing because IT'S NEVER OVER. My mom teaches me that when she reminds me, "You'll never stop worrying about your kids. You never stop mothering. Even when you're a grandma, you're still a mother. I still worry about you kids and pray for you every day. Every single day." Of course she does. Of course I will. Doy. But visualizing her lying in bed each night, imagining where each one of her kids is before she goes to sleep, and praying for each one of us individually, is a powerful image to a mother with a house full of kids.

Attempting to live without regret is heartbreaking, though. It reminds me that miscommunications happen. We all make mistakes and hurt each other, both intentionally and unintentionally. We all become fragmented and distant from each other and from our Heavenly Father. Sin isolates us and breaks down our relationships. Giving in to the reality of choice and agency, which we fundamentally believe in as a tenet of our faith, is giving in to the fact that as mothers we give everything we can—our very best—and then our kids make their own decisions independent of us, and that's it.

But that's *not* it.

The Atonement means something completely different to me as a mother now. The Lord loves my kids more than I do, and just as He suffered and died for me, He suffered and died for my kids, so that we could all be made whole together, forever. We are pieced together again where we were once fragmented. That's the part I fully and finally connected. Hugh Nibley explained the Atonement in this way: "Atonement means 'syntropy'—bringing back to its former state, restoring to its former state. You see, when something breaks down, it becomes disorganized and fractured. At one means unified again—returned to its unity, returned to its former integrity and structure." The Atonement does what we cannot do. It makes up all the rest. It fixes it all. It fills in the cracks. It means we're never alone or isolated. It takes care of everything we've thought of and can't do as well as what we haven't thought of, even after we've done all we can do. The Atonement saves moms from useless worry and more clearly defines the job we have to do.

After I had my first baby, my mom, who was living in Nebraska, came to help me. My mom helped me bathe Miles, which was more difficult than I had ever imagined. Babies are slippery and they don't like to be cold, and there are parts and folds and steps—it's a complicated process and I had only been a mother for a few days. How was

I supposed to figure this out with any confidence? Then, suddenly, she was leaving to go back home to take care of her other children and I felt panicky. I knew I needed to do this on my own and that I could. I was educated and patient, wasn't I? A swirling soup of emotion, uncertainty, and fear came over me. As she left me sitting on the couch in my gauzy muumuu *(I wear muumuus now? Is this who I am now?)*, we were both crying, and she whispered, "Now you know how much I love YOU."

That was a game changer for me. She was crying for *me*. Sure, she would miss her grandchild, and she didn't want to miss a second with him, but I was *her baby*. I got it. The nagging and worry and teaching and wanting to know where I was all the time and what I was doing. Oh, yeah, THAT. I was worried about bathing a newborn and panicked that I might inadvertently harm the baby as I tried, but she knew bathing would be the least of my worries. Game changer. I was incredibly hormonal and, at the same time, coming to the realization that my new son wasn't getting a great deal: I had the best mom, and he had me. Sorry, baby. She, of course, was very encouraging and calmed my fears and expressed great faith in me, as expected, but when she quickly whispered, "Now you know how much I love YOU," it changed the way I saw my own mother. I had assumed that we were both worried about caring for this new baby and keeping him healthy and happy, but I had never considered before this moment that her role as a mother was still in play even though I was "fully grown." My mom was still adjusting to the changing needs of motherhood.

I think about how much I loved my baby at that early mothering moment for me, how much my mom loved me at that middle moment for her, how her mother loved her at the end of her life, and I see how we are connected to each other with the same mother love. I see how all mothers connect to their children and love them so fiercely that it ties us all together as a human family. It's an overwhelming view—this expansive pedigree chart—but this view informs the way I see the world and the gospel. It is not a way of life, or a theory, it *is* love passed down. It's as if my mom had shown me, *I have felt this love for you, and I pass it down to you. Not for any other reason than because I love you and I want to give you everything.* Everyone on the earth who has been or who ever will be is someone's baby, and now I see them with a mother's perspective and I can't ever go back to seeing them any other way. I don't think you have to give birth to feel this way; that's just what it took for me. My mom gave me deep insight about the purpose of life by simply expressing her love for me.

We mothers are often accused by our children of asking too many questions, of being too intrusive, meddling, smothering, and interfering, but that happens because we often err on the side of loving too much instead of not enough. We love too much. *(You're welcome, children.)* Is that even possible? Our job as mothers is to love our kids, to teach them, care for them, and prepare them for the journey ahead because we don't know what that road will look like. One of the hiccups in parenting our kids with a prescriptive list is that we can't predict the future. There is so much I want to teach my kids that, if I make a list, not only does it seems overwhelming (though I wouldn't hate it if they all knew how to play the piano), but it is conditional on so many things that are out of my control: their choices, the choices of others, accidents, surprises, changes in society, technology, and a million other variables. If I can show them how to find answers to their questions (by studying, learning, and seeking personal revelation through prayer and listening to the Holy Ghost), and where to look for guidance (by studying the scriptures, words of the prophets, and worthy mentors), then they can find their own way to find lasting joy, no matter what the path ahead turns out to be.

All of these truths come out of love. There is great truth in love, and I believe it is my job to show my children how to find truth. Hugh Nibley connects love with truth, as well as cheer and thanks, in a meaningful way: "We would say the two things that cover everything are that the Beloved Son is 'full of grace and truth' (John 1:14). You see, truth has nothing false about it. But grace says there is nothing negative about it: self-interest, ulterior motives, scheming, gaining, trying to get ahead, influence, power game, none of that. Grace is the very opposite of that. It's *charis;* our word *cheer* is also related to it, also the Greek *charis,* Latin *gratia. Gratia* means 'thanks.' It means 'a free gift,' a gift you don't ask anything in return for. You feel that way, just as we give things to children not for what they can do for us, but because of love. The tendency is, of course, to render *grace* in the new translations as 'love,' which is right."

The tendency in modern culture is to suppose that the gospel of Jesus Christ is merely a collection of good advice or nice ideas. Worse, some see it as an antiquated way to live or, most cynically, a way to pacify and control the masses. But the gospel of Jesus Christ is the key to motherhood because it's the key to finding truth—not only for our questions in how to raise our particular kids, but for our kids' questions about life, too. The Atonement is real. Not only death is conquered, but all heartache, pain, disappointment (including our expectations), sin, grief, loneliness, and corruption can also be swallowed up. It's the good news that the mission of Jesus Christ has been fulfilled and we all have access to it anytime. And so do our kids.

In 2013, I convinced Miles to run the Provo City Half Marathon with me. I had run a few half marathons before, and he had just finished his first year running with the cross-country team at his high school, so I thought this would be a great mother-son bonding moment I could create with our shared love of running. Of course, I had visions of us doing training runs together, creating inside jokes, and trying out new energy gels and chews together (I love the chocolate ones, he likes the fruity ones), but that didn't really happen. I wanted to run in the mornings, and he wanted to run with his cross-country friends because OF COURSE HE DID. I trained. I trained hard. I stretched and ran and hydrated and created new playlists. Miles ran with his team and didn't sweat it. Literally. When the day of the race came, I thought he would struggle because, in my mind, he hadn't really seemed to have trained hard enough. I was actually a little worried that he wouldn't make it or that he would hurt himself. He wasn't worried at all.

The race started, and he told me I could set the pace and we could run together the whole time, which I was not-so-secretly thrilled by. As we ran together, I took mental pictures of the breathtaking view of the canyon and the tall, skinny man-child running next to me who was growing up at an alarming rate. I just wanted us to enjoy this moment in time together because it would be something that we could always remember. As much as I hated thinking of it, I knew that our time together would be limited. As the oldest, and because of his laid-back nature, Miles doesn't demand much. I wanted to mother him a little, and he let me. I told him when to take water, when to take an energy gel, and he followed along. And then we got to Mile 10.

The last 3.1 miles of a half marathon are the hardest because the thrill and energy are dying—not only for you, but for the other runners around you, which makes for a contagious, zombielike stomping of shufflers. The canyon was beautiful and shaded, but more important it was downhill. After we rounded the curve out of the canopy of trees in the canyon, we had to make our way up a slight incline toward the finish line at blessed Center Street. The last leg of the race took us on a long stretch of flat road on University Avenue for those last 3.1 miles. It was later in the day, it was hot, and we were tired. We could see the finish line, so we knew we were close, but it seemed we would never reach it. Of course we knew we would, but it felt like that last 3.1 miles of the race were taking about ten times as long as the first 10 miles had taken.

My mind goes interesting places on the last bit of a long race. (I think it has something to do with oxygen starvation and my muscles starting to break down. I don't know.) I start to get very emotional, but I reason with my emotions to stay back a bit so I can use every bit of strength to run. A single tear may lead to open sobbing, which would use up the calories and energy my legs need to move. (See? Interesting, nonscientific places.) At that moment in this particular race, I looked over at Miles, and I had a specific thought: *If you put together how much he weighs now with my weight, that equals how much I weighed the day I gave birth to him.* I thought of how, fifteen years ago, I would have thought it was so funny—and weird—what our bodies are able to do and how they change to meet the needs of our kids. Fifteen years ago I was in bed nursing a baby that I had grown inside my body, and I couldn't stop staring at him; now I was running alongside him and I still couldn't stop staring at him. Fifteen years ago I wouldn't have wanted to run two miles, let alone 13.1, and here I was sharing this race with my son. We had both changed so much in ways I could never have imagined.

Then my mind wandered over some of the things that had happened in fifteen years. There were a lot. I had learned to be a mom. I had been humbled and humiliated. I had felt joy and pain in ways I couldn't fully express. I pictured the faces of my children and thought about how I was learning the same lessons over and over again in different forms. Again, I tried to reason with my emotions to stop being so dramatic as I found parallels between running a half marathon with running "the race of life," and how I could use this experience in a church talk sometime. I thought, *It's too obvious a comparison. Too trite.* And then we got to the last mile.

I had expected that we would hold hands when we crossed the finish line together. (I know, stop laughing.) But my brothers and sisters and I had done just that when we had run our first half together, and it was a really meaningful memory for me, and I wanted Miles to have it too. (And it is clearly documented in this book that I love a good dramatic moment, so the fact that I suggested something like this should not come as a shock.) Miles looked over at me, and I told him, "This is the end! This is where we give it all we have!" He smiled—we were both so excited and picking up the pace—and he looked more closely at me and said, "I can't have my MOM beat my time! Do you mind . . . ?" He wanted to run ahead, and he wanted my permission. I was so caught up in the moment: I wanted him to see how fast he could go, so I motioned for him to go on ahead and he took off. It was as if those teenage legs unfolded into these long, gazelle-like strides, and he was gone in a flash. I tried to yell him on, to encourage him, but my heart got stuck in my throat and all that came out was a whisper: *"Go, Miles! You can do it!"*

I tried to catch up with him. In my mind I was going at lightning speed—the fastest I could physically run. (My husband said later that it looked like I was slowing down and I was making a "funny, distorted face" to make him laugh at the end, but the truth is I never saw Topher and I was just running regular. For me. With my regular face.) I was trying to catch up with Miles, to show him that I could keep up and we could finish together, but there was no way.

Then the trite comparison smacked me in the face: There are places coming in which Miles, and each one of my children, will need to go ahead of me. And I want them to go, and I will cheer them on, but I cannot go with them.

Miles met me as I crossed the finish line. Seeing him cheering for *me* was too much, and my reasoning relented to my emotions. He wrapped his long arms around me, and we shared our moment together. The fact was that Miles was prepared, and so was I, but we were prepared in different ways because we had different jobs to do. I had my dramatic moment in the end even though it didn't turn out the way I had imagined it would. It was when I encouraged him forward that I found unexpected joy—joy in a way that I had never before considered.

I know that my kids make their own decisions that will determine who they become and what their race will be like. They run their race and I run my own. I want to be with them for the whole time, but I can't. At the end of the day, that's what I do, exactly: I prepare my kids to run on ahead without me.

Notes

Page 3, "thank you, Malcolm Gladwell": see Malcolm Gladwell, *Outliers: The Story of Success* (2007).

Page 50, "We must be careful": Neal A. Maxwell, *A More Excellent Way* (1967), 130.

Pages 90–91, "snide remarks": Eric D. Snider, "Strolling Down the Street on a Leash," *The Daily Herald,* May 1, 2002, A2.

Page 104, "This authority business": Hugh Nibley, *The Collected Works of Hugh Nibley, vol. 17, Eloquent Witness: Nibley on Himself, Others, and the Temple* (2008), 68.

Page 105, "The fact is": Hugh Nibley, *The Collected Works of Hugh Nibley, vol. 17, Eloquent Witness: Nibley on Himself, Others, and the Temple* (2008), 256–57.

Page 105, "There is a beauty and clarity": Dieter F. Uchtdorf, "Of Things That Matter Most," *Ensign*, November 2010, 20.

Page 121, "The fool doth think he is wise": William Shakespeare, *As You Like It,* act 5, scene 1.

Page 122, "I'm with Marjorie Hinckley": see Virginia H. Pearce, ed., *Glimpses into the Life and Heart of Marjorie Pay Hinckley* (1999), 107.

Page 139, "Life moves pretty fast": John Hughes, *Ferris Bueller's Day Off* (1986 film).

Pages 154–55, "second family": Michael Gurian, *The Wonder of Boys* (1997).

Page 175, "There is no limit": Julie B. Beck, "A 'Mother Heart,'" *Ensign*, May 2004, 77.

Page 177, "Atonement means 'syntropy'": Hugh Nibley, *The*

NOTES

Collected Works of Hugh Nibley, vol. 17, Eloquent Witness: Nibley on Himself, Others, and the Temple (2008), 60.

Page 180, "We would say": Hugh Nibley, *The Collected Works of Hugh Nibley, vol. 17, Eloquent Witness: Nibley on Himself, Others, and the Temple* (2008), 171.

Acknowledgments

My acknowledgments and thanks to the following:

Christopher Layton Clark, Miles, Owen, Phoebe, Hugh, and Margaret for allowing me to write about them and their lives, as well as for their love and support.

Kacy Faulconer and Gina James for reading, editing, and contributing to the ideas in this book.

Laurel Christensen Day for asking in the first place, helping, and encouraging me throughout the entire process.

And especially Dr. Robert Y. Valentine and Shauna Valentine for their enthusiastic support in everything I do, including but not limited to writing this book, and for showing me how meaningful, rewarding, and fun parenthood can be.

About the Author

Lisa Valentine Clark graduated with a B.S. in English from Brigham Young University. She was part of the sketch comedy/improv troupe "The Garrens" in Provo from 1995 to 2000, and co-founded the theater-as-improv troupe "The Thrillionaires." She has done a variety of voiceover and acting work in independent features, including "Gracie" in the award-winning webseries *Pretty Darn Funny,* which she also writes and produces. Lisa spends most of her time in Provo with her husband, Christopher Clark. They are the parents of five children who seem to make up a unique comedy troupe all their own.